Romance and
MURDER
in
Bensonhurst

Written by Elliot M. Rubin

Copyright January 2013
United States Library of Congress
ISBN 09901306031
ISBN 9780991306039

Acknowledgements

I would like to thank my late father, Herman S. Rubin, for his inspiration and encouragement to write.

He wrote essays, prayers, and poetry his whole life and his writings are treasured by those who have read them.

Also, I want to thank my beloved grandmother, Bessie Greenberg, for giving me the gift of creativity and imagination. Her lunchtime stories of Moishe Kapoya when I was a child stirred my creative mind to picture the story and think.

And finally, I want to thank my dear wife Laura who is an avid reader and whom I love very much. Again her total disinterest in what I write just stirred me on to write more.

Introduction

This novel consists of ***disassociated*** short stories of romance, murder, and organized crime emanating in Bensonhurst Brooklyn. There is a backdrop of family sagas that begin in Europe and come together in the last chapter in Brooklyn New York.

Spanning three generations, with the main and peripheral characters mostly female, it centers around three sisters, and how their myopic world swirls around them and their families.

The family tree

Theresa Avila - Gaetano
1
Anna Marie – Mario
1
Gina Marie – Rocco

Mary Catherine – Carlo

Carmen –Nick

Chapter 1-

His heart is beating faster. It is pounding in his chest as he walked determinately through the forest trying to keep a distance from her.

The snow laid a thick blanket of white on the frozen ground in Latgale Park, Latvia. The quiet of the forest is deafening to him as he stood there for a very brief moment.

Silence is his only weapon of defense, yet it deprived him of exhaling loudly and trying to catch his breath. Beads of sweat are racing down his face and freezing as soon as they hit the frigid winter air. His eyes are frozen wide open and searching ahead as he moves forward, deeper into the park's forest.

Looking up he saw a hawk flying above the wintry canopy of trees also hunting, the difference being he is the prey and not the hunter like the hawk.

Dashing as fast as he can he moves from tree to tree trying to find a place to hide. But the snow on the ground is announcing his every move as he continues forward.

Desperate, he spots a frozen lake ahead, and must quickly decide if he should try to cross it before he is found. He approaches the edge, but he doubts if the ice will hold him.

***

Peter is a middle-aged chemist at the Riga Techni Institute in Riga, Latvia. He is not married and is a bit of a nerd although some would consider him handsome but quiet.

He is working on a secret formula for the Russian Military to use in chemical warfare. Although chemical warfare is not officially sanctioned Peter is given a grant through the Kremlin (and KGB) to research a use for a very dangerous substance.

He is doing groundbreaking work and achieved the outcome that the military desired. After he sent the chemical to the Kremlin, with his notes, a woman who is visiting Riga approached him.

They met on a bus. She flirted and started a conversation with him. The woman spoke fluent Russian and is also a chemist in East Germany. The young looking woman is semi vacationing in the Baltic's on a goodwill tour sponsored by the East German government. But what he did not know is the CIA is also paying her to go on the tour to meet him, and get his notes.

They enjoy a nice short conversation on the bus, and she asked him if he knew of any good restaurants in Riga that she could go have a tasty meal. He said he knew of a very good one, and offered to escort her to dinner that evening.

The two decided to meet at a famous traditional Latvian restaurant that night and have dinner on Kalkuliela [Kalkul Street].

Peter picked her up at her hotel that evening at six o'clock and escorted her to dinner. He ordered a traditional Latvian dish of baked pork ribs with sautéed sauerkraut and boiled potatoes. His date ordered fish (perch) cooked in milk with boiled potatoes. They both enjoyed the food and joked with each other a lot. She is having a good time, and the conversation flowed freely.

After dinner, they talked some more and ordered a few drinks. She told him if he worked in East Germany he could earn almost the equivalent of three million rubles. She whispered to him "Why not go on vacation next month to East Berlin, and I will meet you and introduce you to my company." He thought about it for a second but made no decision.

After a few more drinks together he invited her back to his apartment and they stayed the rest of the evening in his bed.

What he did not know is since he is working on sensitive matters for the military, the KGB are silently watching his every move, and recording all his private conversations.

They heard her ask him again to come to East Germany to work, between their sexual encounters that night in his bed. His home is bugged, and everything he said is recorded by the KGB. The military could not afford to take any chances that he would defect to the west, and take their secrets with him. His work is finished, and now he is dispensable.

The KGB sent Olga Levovna Levinsky to Riga to silence him.

Olga is trained in all types of hand and weapons combat to kill immediately without compassion or thinking. It is to be second nature and instinctive in order for her to be successful. She also is a top marksman with a pistol and rifle.

The following week Olga arrived in Riga and went to see him at his laboratory at the University. A black car drove up to the University entrance, and Olga stepped out from the rear door.

She walked into the building and turned to her right to go up one flight of stairs. The wooden banister had the finish rubbed off from many years of students holding on. The stairway is well lit but its age is showing. The paint is starting to peel off but no university funds were spent on repainting the hallways. The government priorities determined other places to spend their money.

Olga is wearing a dark navy skirt with a light blue blouse under a full-length mink sable coat.

When she entered the lab and asked to see Peter everyone stopped working. They all started to stare at her. Peter usually did not get any guests walking in asking for him, especially someone so good looking and obviously well off. A secretary excused herself and offered to go tell him there is a guest in the lab.

"Hello, I am Peter," he said when he entered the room to meet her.

"Hello Peter, my name is Olga. Is there a place where we can talk privately?" she asked.

"Yes, yes, over here…in this side office I have" as he pointed to a walnut stained wooden and glass door at the back of the lab.

After they entered and sat Olga took off her coat. She draped it over the back of the chair with the fur facing away from her body. The richly lined silk interior faced out.

Olga sat facing him while crossing her long legs so her skirt was drawn up a little exposing her left thigh. He sat down opposite her and caught himself staring at her legs. She expected that reaction. Olga does nothing unless there is a reason for it.

"Peter, I am here on private business," she told him. "I need you to meet me in Rezekne, outside of Riga next week. The supervisor of my company wants to meet you, and he has an offer for you. You can make a lot of money in only one week of work in Moscow" she continued.

"How did you hear about me?" Peter said. He wondered how this rich woman and her supervisor knew of him.

She laughed a small laugh when she heard his question. "My company does some work for the military. You were highly recommended by General Kominski at the Kremlin. He said you just finished a project for him, and I should get in contact with you" Olga answered. She knew Peter would recognize that name.

"Of course, you realize General Kominski does not want his name mentioned once you accept this position. He will be paying you directly in rubles, personally" she assured him. This satisfied his curiosity and relaxed his anxiety.

"You are to meet me at the location where the Latgale Music Festival holds their annual gathering. I will then take you to meet my supervisor inside the park" she continued.

"This Monday meet me there at noon. I will be waiting for you" she said as she stood and put on her flowing mink coat.

"It is a pleasure to meet you, Olga," Peter said as he stood to say goodbye to her, and shake her hand.

"Here is some money to get to Rezekne next week" as she gave him a hand full of rubles. He took them and stood there holding them. Peter stared at her as she slowly bent backward to slip one arm, then the next, into her mink coat, pushing her chest outwards so as to catch his glare.

Then Olga walked out of the University and back into the waiting black car which took her to a local hotel. There she unpacked and had a few days to kill until next week in Latgale Park.

The park is actually a large forest with lakes and many hills. It is widely known in the Baltic region.

***

On Sunday Peter left for Rezekne and he decided he would not be late for such an important meeting.

If General Kaminski recommended him he knew there would be interesting work for him. He could use some extra money as it only made things more interesting.

Peter was hesitant to work for the military at first. Some of his closest friends told him that the KGB would be watching his every move, but he did not think of it that way. It is a patriotic thing he did for Mother Russia, and he is proud to do it.

The bus arrived at the entrance of the park about a half hour early, and he waited for her to arrive. The weather is below freezing and very cold with his breadth appearing as a cloud in the air.

Exactly at noon, a large black car drove up, and the rear door opened. Olga put her right leg out of the door to leave. As she stood her short wool jacket opened, her skirt blew up from the wind, and Peter saw a pistol holstered to the top of her right leg, near her thigh.

At that moment he realized there is no job offer for him. This is a setup, and he is going to be killed. He turned and ran into the forest with Olga following him about fifty feet behind.

She sensed he must have figured it out when he bolted for the forest. Slowly she started to chase him into the park. She did not have to draw her gun yet, she had time.

First, she needs to catch up to him. Following him is easy as his footprints in the snow give away his every move.

Peter is walking as fast as he could. He is not in shape, and physically exhausted as he approached the edge of a lake when he stopped. He leaned his head against a large tree to rest for a moment. He did not exercise in years, ever since his youth. This is too much exertion for his body. His nostrils are flared out to gather in the ice-cold air and bring it to his lungs. He can feel his heart beating about to burst out of his chest from exertion. Peter knew what would happen to him if she caught up to him. He heard stories about other people, never expecting this could happen to him.

Olga saw him in the distance standing there against a tree. Slowly she walked up to the tree, the hunter's prey realizing the chase is over, and she stood in front of Peter.

"What did I do?" Peter asked, choking out the words from exhaustion and exasperation.

"I do not know what you did. Nor do I care" Olga calmly answered him.

"Please" he begged her, with his arms outstretched begging for mercy. "I take care of my elderly mother in Riga. Please let me go" he said as the sweat from running beaded up and froze on his forehead. "I will give you whatever I have, please" he begged to her, pleading for his life.

"I cannot do that" she answered.

Olga took a few steps back and stopped. Looking directly at him, staring at his face, she showed no emotion. Her eyes riveted on him, not blinking. This was business.

She lifted up her skirt and took out her pistol. Calmly she raised her arm and pointed the barrel of the gun directly at Peter.

The bullets flew into the center of his chest. Blood spurt out as the impact lifted him slightly into the air. His head rocketed backward and his legs flew out from under him. The tree acted as a backdrop as his body slammed into it.

The gunshots echoed through the forest, but no one is there to hear it. In mid-winter, only the wild animals roam through the park.

Peter slumped to the ground, the tree behind him giving support to his lifeless body. The warm blood oozed out of the wounds into the cold air and causing it to vaporize in a cloud of steam that rose from his body.

Olga calmly holstered her gun, and slowly walked out of the park leaving him there for the wolves to feast. She sat in the waiting black car which took her back to the hotel in Riga.

When she walked into her hotel room, waiting there for her to arrive was her handler, Viktor. He was much older than her and oversaw her progress in the KGB since she started.

Olga matter of factly gave her verbal report the job is finished. The two of them kissed, and then went downstairs to have dinner. Afterwards, they went back to the room to spend the evening together.

Chapter 2 -

As Carmen walked slowly to the well-worn grey limestone steps in front of the church her family attends, she had many thoughts racing through her mind. She did not notice the spiraling turrets of a replicated medieval church that were reaching for the heavens above her, or the dark storm clouds gathering in the sky.

How would she start; what should she say first? It wouldn't be easy for her to talk about her troubled marriage. It took her many months to get up the courage to come here.

Being raised in a devout Catholic Italian family caused her to have severe secret emotional conflicts about her feelings of self, and her forbidden thoughts.

In her mind, her sexuality was in question. She had these dreams, these emotions that she felt she could no longer control. She realized that she had to talk to someone.

Today she was dressed rather conservatively; the jeans and tee shirts were left at home. After all, she was entering a holy place and that was how she was raised.

Her mother and grandmother were extremely conservative in their dress. They only wore black after their husbands had died but Carmen's husband was not dead and she wore fashionable clothing. And even if he were dead she would not wear black. Her mother never dated after her husband's death or even thought of doing so.

They were born in the old country and never forgot the customs they knew from there. Being in America didn't change things for them. They just transplanted their Southern Italian ways to Brooklyn and continued like they never left Italy. They always said they were from Italy, and not Sicily, because it sounded higher class. But they were originally from Palermo, Sicily.

Her grandmother, Theresa Avila, had been in this country for many years and still barely spoke English. Theresa was raised in Sicily by her Sicilian parents but as a young woman lived in Northern Africa with her husband. But in this neighborhood, she was able to work and get by just speaking Italian. Here there was no need for her to learn English.

Yet years later here was her granddaughter Carmen about to talk to a priest about a marriage in free fall.

In old style Catholic Italian homes you suffered with a bad marriage. Her mother did, but Carmen had other thoughts about that. Not that her mother had a terrible marriage, but Carmen felt she was held back in her life. That her mother had suffered in silence.

That was one reason Carmen had decided to come today and talk about it with Father Donovan.

Divorce was unheard of in her family. But she had had enough and if she could not get satisfaction from the priest, then she would do what she had to.

A person would be excommunicated from the church and their souls would go to hell when they died if they divorced. That is what she learned since she was a little girl going to a strict parochial school in Brooklyn.

The nuns inculcated that into them. You never even thought of divorce, or if you did it vanished from your mind very quickly. The scowl on the nun's faces when the subject of divorce came up shooed away any thoughts of divorce from young impressionable minds. But adult minds think differently when their hormones start to come into play.

She had tried her best to make the marriage work, but it only became harder and harder to do. Finally, she had had enough. She had to talk to someone about it.

They were married for five years and it was only after the first six months had passed did she discover the secret her husband Nicky had kept from her.

There were hints, but he never told her outright, and she never realized them until finally her suspicions were confirmed.

And she would not dare speak to tell her husband about her secrets, either. But today she was going to talk to the priest and tell him everything, and finally get it off her chest.

***

Bensonhurst Brooklyn is an Italian American enclave.

It is home to many organized crime families and the borough is also known as the borough of churches. It seems that on almost every block or so there is a church. Some of them are extremely large and they are all filled every Sunday for Mass.

On occasion, even the organized crime wise guys go to church. It looks good to the community that they are some kind of honest person who believes in God. Yet they make their living causing misery on many of the very people who are in also church that Sunday.

The heart of the area is 86th street and the elevated subway that runs over it has become an icon of the area. Standing under the tracks you cannot but hear the deafening sound of the steel wheels on the tracks as the trains roar overhead. You can't help not to look up at the noise, it is so loud. Clickity clacks bounce off the streets and echo in your ears when the train's steel wheels rumble overhead. If it is the first time you are there you are amazed when you look up and see railroad tracks only forty feet or so over your head. It is an eerie feeling.

Small local shops of every kind, with extra wide sidewalks for the hordes of people to walk on, line the street for miles and miles just below the elevated trains.

Every bank in the city is also located in the area. They are all fighting for people's money to be put into their branches.

There is a lot of cash floating around this section of Brooklyn. It has become somewhat of an art form on how to hide money and not pay sales tax or income tax. Plus the illegal activities of certain local citizens lend itself to a cash only society.

Of the tens of thousands of people who live in the Bensonhurst area, according to the IRS, most of them earn an average living. Yet many of them drive expensive cars, wear Rolexes, and have more gold hanging from their necks, fingers, and wrists than the Federal Reserve has in their vaults.

It's their thing.

The educated ones will hide their racial prejudices yet they have as much bling as the minorities in Bed Stuy that they rant and rave about negatively.

Some of the citizens in Bensonhurst complain that the minorities in New York live exclusively on welfare and don't work. Yet many of them who do complain the most also don't work. At least they do not work legally.

The homes are for the most part sturdy middle class looking houses. All are well maintained by their hard-working owners. But if you enter a lot of them you are amazed at the marble floors, the expensive furniture, and the solid brass crystal chandeliers hanging in the hallway. This is organized crime's neighborhood. Baroque rules here.

A lot of the women and young girls wear their hair teased up, flowing down their backs, and wear stilettos that push their rumps high into the air.

Tight pants or skirts are almost mandatory, along with tight blouses and brassieres that push everything up and out for all to see, and admire. The buttons are unbuttoned two or three down. Exposure is the look of the day, whether it is warm out or cool.

Their nails are long and polished. And they all have either gold or diamond nameplates on a chain hung around their necks, just below their heavily carved and diamond encrusted crosses, which are resting on their surgically enhanced pushed up breasts.

As you travel down on McDonald Avenue and get closer to Coney Island and the Belt Parkway, you come into the Gravesend Section of Brooklyn.

That is where the hit men dump the bodies of their dead victims. At night it is not uncommon to have a stolen car stop, a door opens, and a body is pushed out onto the street.

All a funeral home has to do is patrol there on any given weekend morning and it's almost a guarantee they'll find a body laying somewhere in the area. That's a fact.

The mob will either dump the bodies in Gravesend or bring it to one of their favorite funeral homes if they really do not want the body found. They own a few funeral homes in Brooklyn; and one each in Manhattan and Long Island.

Their favorite one though is the Fattachie Family Funeral Home on 48th Street and Thirteenth Avenue in the Boro Park section of Brooklyn.

The Fattachie funeral homes have a few specially constructed custom-made coffins with an elevated platform that they put their victim under. Over him goes whoever is really being buried that day, somebody's Aunt Tilley or Uncle Louie, or whomever.

The FBI will have to dig up hundreds of thousands of bodies of everyone's aunts, uncles, grandparents and other relatives of noncriminal people, buried all over the city if they want to find a particular missing person. This type of criminal burial is only for very important bodies that someone doesn't want to be found, ever.

In the warmer weather, the men in Bensonhurst wear sleeveless undershirts, flexing their biceps, and the girls wear teeny tight fitting tops with pushup bras and cutoff jeans where the bottom of their rear end hangs out. It is a kind of uniform of sorts.

The small mom and pop shops sell everything from the basics that are needed for everyday living like bakeries and shoe stores too hard to find delicious imported delicacies brought in directly from Italy.

The Bensonhurst area also has in existence some of the only old-fashioned butcher shops left in operation that has disappeared from almost every community in America. The meats are hand cut for you, and fresh is the only word used.

Only in the Orthodox Jewish communities of Boro Park and Williamsburg can you also find these kinds of butcher shops. The meats are all hand cut and weighed right in front of you, not prepackaged in plastic like they do in a supermarket.

Ask for a special cut and they will go into the walk-in refrigerator and bring out a large piece of meat, and custom cut it for you at that moment.

You have to look in a library's picture archives if you want to see other butcher shops. They are all gone. But here, in this neighborhood, you can actually experience it.

Sawdust is liberally strewn on the floor where the customers walk so any spilled blood is absorbed and can be easily cleaned and swept away later.

The brown paper that the meat is wrapped in is on a roller behind the counter where you can see the butcher carefully wrap your purchase himself.

If you are standing in front of the counter you can actually see the sirloin steak ground into chop meat right in front of your eyes, or a large slab of beef liver carved to any size portion for your dinner that night.

On the side streets, hidden away, are the slaughterhouses that usually do chickens and ducks. If you bring in a pig from an upstate farm they will slaughter it and cut it into steaks and quarters for you. It is not uncommon for a few families to chip in and they will share a pig; otherwise, it is too large a quantity for one family. A lot of people have freezer chests in their basement to store such large quantities of meat. Sometimes the freezer, if needed, also serves in a criminal sort of way on occasion.

Hanging in the deli windows for everyone to see is the imported Italian cheeses lined from wall to wall in the front of the store. The thought of some of those imports can stir the saliva in almost anyone who enjoys specialty cheeses.

For Christmas and Easter Sunday meals the shops bring in for sale dozens of skinned and gutted rabbits. It is considered a delicacy, especially the head.

Many organized crime members that live in Bensonhurst also donate a lot of their money to their parishes to build rectories, schools and help support the local church. It is a way to give back a little of what they took illegally.

That fact gets frequently overlooked on Sundays in church when they come in with their wives and children, or if they make a very large cash donation.

All of the new wings to the school buildings are financed by them.

Also, custom built brick parsonages for the nuns and priests are donated by dirty money. But atonement is given, either by the priests by not asking important questions and ignoring where the money came from, or in their own minds when they give their blood money to the church.

Maybe it also is a way to clear their consciences, if they have one.

Many of them are psychopaths and have no remorse for the lives they destroy. But it looks good to give to the church. And the community recognition is a big ego booster too. They are treated with respect.

Respect is a very big thing to them, very important.

If someone disrespects the wrong person things can happen to them. And it usually hurts a lot.

***

As Carmen continued to walk to the church the concrete sidewalk felt like it was made of glue. Her legs grew heavy and tired from her depression. She had a lot on her mind but felt the only way to relieve her mental anguish was in her church. The teachings, that the nun's put into her head, still played a strong part in her depression.

Slowly Carmen opened the large, richly carved, oak stained wooden doors that almost every church in Brooklyn has. It seems the bigger the doors, the larger the church. They were well oiled and they opened very easily as she walked into the cool, darkish vestibule. She smelled the slightest scent of incense as she stood there for a moment and adjusted her eyes to the dim lighting.

The only light was from the stained glass above her but the storm clouds kept everything dark inside.

Standing there she could see just ahead of her the rows of candles burning by the side door in the front of the church. There was an elderly lady dressed in black kneeling by them offering a prayer and lighting a candle.

On the right side of the church was the foreboding confessional booth.

Growing up she used to go in there, especially when she was in high school. The nuns insisted on it and took the high school girls to confessional monthly; sometimes more if they thought it was needed. This was their way of controlling them, and also guiding them, to stay on the right path in life as they saw it. Sometimes it worked for a little while, but mostly it did not.

But Carmen never confessed what the church would consider a major sin.

That she felt was between her and her Jesus. It was none of the priests business what she considered private and not for anyone to hear, or know about except her. But today, in church, it would be different when she spoke to the priest in his office. The burden of a disappointing marriage was finally too hard for her to keep to herself.

Behind the main altar; which was located in the front of the church, all of the church offices were located in a long brick encased hallway with minimum lighting.

As she slowly walked down the center of the wooden pews Carmen stopped in the middle for a moment of silence.

She looked up. The ceiling was so high it seemed like it almost touched heaven. It never looked so high before, but today it did. Everything in the church now jumped out at her, at this moment in her life; probably due to nerves. Now nothing in the darkish church went unnoticed.

A red carpet ran between the pews from the back of the church to the raised altar in the front, right down the middle of the church. There was very little padding under the carpet, only the hard concrete floor; that made each step harder and harder under the weight of her thoughts.

Her knees started to shake a little from anticipation. They felt weak so she stood for a moment near an end pew and held on for a second or two. She knew she had to continue forward or she would never be able to do this again. It took a lot of courage for her to come here today, she could not back out.

She said a small prayer, under her breath, as she proceeded to the priest's office situated behind the altar and down the hall... "Jesus please help me to do this. I have to tell somebody," she silently prayed to herself.

Carmen thought that perhaps her holy Jesus would hear her prayer and give her the emotional strength she needed now. Or even the Holy Mother Mary who was holding the baby Jesus in her arms, close to her chest, that she saw on the sculpture by the side of the altar. She searched for the inner strength to continue.

She had nowhere to turn, and no one to turn to, except for her priest, Father Donovan. Her faith in the church, she believed, would help her in this her time of need and desperation.

Carmen was in her late twenties and had very soft features. Her olive skin and her small thin-lipped mouth did not betray the fact that she was of Italian heritage. Not like her older sisters who were big boned, had fuller mouths and were very loud, outgoing women. They wore their hair teased as high as it could go and their long wavy hair flowed back down their necks and over their shoulders.

Her two sisters were married and each had a few kids.

Gina Marie was the oldest and the broadest. Her hips and thighs were exceedingly wide and she wobbled when she walked. Her shape skipped right past curvy and went directly to triangular after she had kids. She was the oldest sister and was married to Rocco for ages.

He worked for a construction company as a driver for Paulie, the owner.

Rocco would sometimes work nights driving him around to different pizza places in the city that he also owned. That is what he told her, but the New York Police Department had other ideas on what he did for a living.

Gina Marie never thought it was strange that he never spoke about where he was on the phone or about his day when he was in their house. He would speak about it only if they were on a subway car or walking on the avenue. She just never gave it any thought what so ever. People who knew her could describe her as being simple and accepting things at face value as she did them.

Some folks in the neighborhood said that Paulie was a mob boss and was connected to organized crime. So did the police. But nothing was ever proven. They were just whispers and rumors.

Mary Catherine was the middle daughter. She was a larger boned, tall woman but much thinner than Gina Marie and very shapely. She wore her light brown hair down past her shoulder to mid back. Mary Catherine was very striking with her very light blue/gray penetrating eyes when she looked directly at you. Her gaze reminded many of a wolf's blue/gray eyes, they went right through you.

Her clothes were always tight fitting and she showed what she had when she went out.

Mary Catherine was also married for many years and had two sons, Frankie and Anthony. They were currently out on bail waiting to go to court on a federal felony charge of stealing diamonds that were shipped from Amsterdam.

It seems the boys made a wrong turn on the Belt Parkway and ended up at Kennedy Airport inside a freight terminal. When they exited their car asking for directions someone, supposedly unknown to them, placed some boxes of imported jewelry into the trunk of their car; and they then tried to drive away.

The FBI is saying something totally different due to some videotape they were said to have from the terminal's security cameras. Only time and a trial will tell. That is if the videotapes are not somehow misplaced. Things like that do happen on occasion.

The tapes have to go to an evidence locker from the security room at the airport and sometimes they never get to where they are supposed to go. They say it is human error and maybe they were destroyed by accident. It was known to happen; especially if the security firm that was hired by the airport is controlled by Paulie.

Mary Catherine was beside herself with worry. But her late husband Carlo had previously hired a very good lawyer for some business dealings he had; so she used him for the boys. He had received the lawyer's name from his brother-in-law Rocco.

He knew that if Rocco recommended him then that was the lawyer to use.

Carmen, unlike her sisters, was a petite girl and carried herself well. Her dark black hair is tied back into a ponytail. She rarely lets it down except at night when she goes to bed. That's because her husband Nicky had requested that. He liked her with her hair down. At least that was what he said when they were first married. But over time things had changed between them, and not for the better.

When she opened the door to Father Donovan's office she saw him sitting behind his big, dark, wooden desk reading the newspaper.

He must have been in his late forties or early fifties but looked much younger. Only the touch of gray in his salt and pepper hair gave away his maturity, and it was very becoming. He had been a priest for over twenty something years already.

His desk was over half a century old and was bought way before the church was redone forty years ago. It showed its age and use. The rub marks on the top of the old solid oak wooden desk were able to be seen where all the previous priest's arms had rested on it over the years. Many priests had used this desk, too many to name.

Father Donovan had been an athlete when he was younger before he had a calling for the priesthood.

The toned muscles were still there as he went to the parish gym to work out every day. Chiseled facial features foretold the tight abdomen beneath his black jacket and starched white collar.

In high school, he was on the track and football teams. In the two years, he played on the varsity squads his school came in either first or second each year in their division.

Carmen entered and apologized for being a little late. She almost stuttered, as she was so nervous. She spoke very quickly and breathlessly.

"I live ina two fam-ly house wit my muther liv'in upstairs. My muther stopped cook'in for ah while an she came down before I left. She had tried to start a convo-sation with me…but I wuz on my way out and did'int want to miss dis appointment with youse…. I knew my muther wuz home cause I could smell dah garlic coming down dah staircase ta my apartment." I said "Ma, I have to go wit Nicole downtown and I'm late. Talk to youse later, an I left inner hurry ta get here" she quickly told the priest. Her nerves were showing now and it made her uncomfortable.

Her mother, Anna Marie, was making her own tomato gravy, tomato sauce to non-old world Italians, and had it simmering when she decided to take a rest.

It was a little unusual for Carmen to be going out dressed that nicely in the middle of the day, her mother thought, especially on her day off from work. She never wore makeup as she was blessed with a naturally beautiful skin tone and face. But Anna Marie didn't think to say anything about it.

Today Carmen was wearing a light gray skirt with a very small pattern and a beige blouse under a matching jacket.

She didn't dare tell her mother where she was actually going, and why. Too many questions would bring answers nobody really wanted to hear, or know about. Silence was the only right way to speak at that moment.

When she entered the priest's office, her eyes caught his, and they looked at each other.

For a brief moment, nothing was said by either of them.

There were unspoken words communicated between them by their gaze.

It was not the first time that happened to the both of them. This would take place every Sunday at Mass when they would see each other, as he placed a wafer on her tongue. He would look down at her and gently smile with an ever slight twinkle in his eye. She felt secure in his presence. His maturity appealed to her, on many levels.

Carmen sensed something when he smiled at her at Mass, and it stirred feelings she knew she should not have.

As she entered the priest's office she stopped for a moment and looked at him. Her heart started to beat faster and her legs felt weak. Carmen's nerves were unsettling her composure. The last time she felt this way was her first sexual encounter. Quickly she sat down.

Father Donovan just sat there and dared not say what he thought, nor would she. He was a priest, but still human, and had to try to control his emotions and feelings as best he could.

Carmen sat down in the faded, crinkled brown leather chair that was in front of his desk. It showed the weathered look of leather that had been sat in for years on end. If the chair could only talk, the stories it would tell. The many tears that fell on it and had carved tiny stains into the softness of the leather were evident. The chair was the holder of unwritten stories of people with troubles who sought solace, comfort, and answers in their holy church.

The office itself was painted in a beige color that had faded over the years and needed a new coat of paint. A few photographs were hanging on the walls of the church when it was built decades before. They were so old they were in black and white. The only colored pictures were of the more recent Popes.

How could she tell him her thoughts, her desires? He could not see her knees shaking with nervousness on the other side of the desk.

How can she even begin speaking of her marriage when she had these unholy feelings?

Father Donovan broke the silence and mentioned how nice the weather was yesterday. Spring had finally come to Brooklyn and the flowers were blooming.

A new start to life was happening outside. Yet inside the church, flowers of a marriage were wilting.

The evil spirit was watching and waiting. The Devil was in the wings ready to alight into the bowels of the church. It was only a matter of time and opportunity. Satan would not be denied. He just had to wait and work on their desires. This he knew how to do very well, and he did not wait to start working.

Finally, after a brief awkward moment of silence, Father Donovan had stood and walked to his office door. He gently, but firmly, closed the door to his office but did not lock it…yet.

As he turned to go back to his desk he saw her legs shaking and realized she was very nervous. He stopped behind her chair and gently rubbed her shoulders.

"Relax," he told her. "You are in good hands now. Everything will be okay. You'll see" he said with a lifting lilt to his voice and a smile on his face.

Softly massaging her shoulders and neck her body started to slowly slump into the leather chair and her legs stopped moving. She could feel the tenseness easing as he rubbed her shoulders. His strong masculine hands massaged her neck muscles as she started to close her eyes. She felt a tingling in the pit of her stomach and a longing she knew she should have.

When he felt her relax he looked down at her from above and smirked ever so slightly.

He stopped rubbing her neck, walked around to the back of the desk, and sat slowly down into his chair. He haltingly outstretched his arm across the top of the desk and gently held her hand to comfort her.

She felt a sexual tension towards the priest that she had tried to deny to herself for months.

Softly, slowly…she started to speak.

"Fadder, I have some problems in my life an I don't know what ta do," she said, barely above a whisper. Her voice was lightly quivering with nervousness.

Carmen was confident that she was protected. She felt that the secret to her marriage would not be betrayed. He was a priest and she knew that whatever they spoke about was privileged and a sacred communication. Her mother would never learn what she was about to tell him.

After five years she now was facing her demons and finally felt secure and somewhat at ease.

The storm clouds outside let loose and a torrential rain started to fall pelting the windows with small pings of sound. Strong winds swept through the leaves outside and swirled around the strong outer limestone walls of the church.

Inside Father, Donovan was holding her hand in his as he gently moved his thumb over the back of her hand. The softness of his masculine strokes reassured her in a strange way. Although it was an innocent gesture she felt a sexual pull towards him. It was a strange feeling. She was about to begin telling him about her best girlfriend Nicole, and her husband Nick, and how her emotional life was in turmoil.

Just then there was a knock at the door and it was elderly Sister Bernadette reminding him through the door "there is a choir practice that afternoon with the elementary boys' choir from the school".

He stood up from behind the desk and went to open the door and tell her he would be there. "I didn't forget Sister, I will be there as usual after school lets out," he said to her.

Father Donovan stepped back from the open door as he watched Sister Bernadette walk away. He quietly closed the door again.

Slowly he went to sit down behind his desk to continue the conversation. But he stopped a few feet behind her chair, and turned back around and locked the door to his office.

"Now where were we?" he asked her as he started to rub her shoulders again.

Chapter 3 -

In 1911 when Italy won the North African territories from the Ottoman Empire after a bloody war, it brought over many of its best industries to set up shop there. It was hoping to Italianize the country.

Besides Fiat building a new factory to employ the population, the Italian government also started to build a rail system in Libya. That was when Anna Marie's parents were sent there to help supervise its construction.

The land was barren, flat and hot with sand everywhere. The coastal cities were a blend of small two and three-story high buildings, but mostly small buildings with tall sand colored walls ten feet high to keep the world out and the women in. Even more so than Europe, Islamic society was extremely male-dominated.

Coming from the Palermo Sicily part of Italy, they were used to warm summer weather and it was hoped that the desert heat would not be too much for them. But needing a better job Anna Marie's father, Gaetano, jumped at the chance to improve his situation and provide for his family.

He was able to take his wife Theresa Avila and young daughter, Anna Marie, with him to North Africa.

Theresa was a small woman with strong Sicilian blood flowing through her veins and beautiful olive colored skin. Her features were very fine and petite with dark brown hair that flowed down her back. When you talked to her you saw the flame in her eyes and knew that she was alive and full of life.

She had a fiery personality and was not to be fooled with. Yet with Gaetano, she was soft and kind.

He was her first and only love and he met her just by chance.

Gaetano was from Naples and was traveling through Sicily with his buddies one summer when he was an engineering student.

He and a few of his friends had decided to go to a local dance at a cantina one night in Palermo, and that was where he actually met her.

The cantina was filled with young single men and women. There were wine and music and people were dancing and singing and just having a festive time.

They had been introduced that night by a cousin of Gaetano's who lived in Palermo and knew Theresa from school. When they saw each other it was love at first sight.

The moon was smiling and the stars were dancing along with them.

The couple danced, drank wine and laughed for hours that night. After a few hours, Theresa asked if they could go outside to cool off. They were both hot from the humidity and the ceiling fan was not doing a great job.

As they left and turned to rest on the side of the building, Gaetano turned towards her and kissed her lightly on the cheek. She put her left hand on the back of his head and drew him close to her. They started to breathe heavily and Theresa took him by the hand and they walked a little bit until they came to a field in the back.

There was no light except for the reflection of the moon. She turned to him and undid her dress and it fell onto the field. She bent down and gently sat on the dress totally naked. Quickly he sat down next to her and both embraced with kisses and groping.

He took off his clothes and as they both would lie back on the soft grass, it cushioned their bodies ever so softly.

Gaetano became her first and only love.

Time quickly flew by that night and when they were finished Gaetano asked if he could call her the next day. She said yes and he made it a point to write down the address so he would not forget it when they came back to the cantina. She made sure he wrote it down. Theresa did not want the wine to ruin a good thing and have him forget the address.

As they parted that night he took her to the side of the dance floor and taking her hand, pulled her close to him and kissed her. She knew at that very moment he would be her husband. Their passion was still warm as they parted that night.

For the rest of the summer they dated, and together went to the beach with their friends. They had romantic walks at night in the local parks, sitting together on the sand on a blanket at dusk listening to the waves, and having someone in your arms that you cared for very much made this a romance that would last forever.

He decided not to travel any further that summer with his friends and spent the rest of the time in Palermo with her. It was more than a summer romance; it was a very rare commodity, true love.

The summer was speeding away and September was just around the corner and he would have to go back. He had to finish school as he was studying to be an engineer.

One evening when they were alone and not with friends, Gaetano finally asked Theresa to marry, and she said yes.

He had taken her to the edge of the bay. Walking hand in hand with the city lights shining behind them, and as the sun was setting and the cool evening sea breeze was coming in, he turned to her.

Gently he took hold of both of her hands and brought her close to him for a kiss. Then he said he wanted to spend the rest of his life with her and asked if she would marry him. But first, she told him he had to ask her father, which he readily agreed to do.

Before dinner the following night Gaetano sat down outside next to her father and politely asked for his approval of their marriage. Theresa's mother is informed ahead of time and ensured that her husband gave the correct approval to Gaetano. Theresa's world was at peace.

Gaetano telegraphed his family in Naples and they made arrangements to come to Sicily and meet her family. They had heard a lot about Theresa's family from Gaetano and it was all good news. They were excited to meet the girl of his dreams. His mother was so excited about the engagement that she couldn't wait to meet her. She packed their suitcases immediately and the next day they traveled to Sicily before the summer officially ended.

The families joyously met one night for dinner at Theresa's family's house to arrange a wedding and discuss a dowry.

Her family lived on a hill at the edge of Palermo. It was a modest house and her mother and father made Gaetano and his family welcome in it.

For dinner, Theresa's mother cooked lasagna that was absolutely delicious because she used the fresh cheese she had made that morning herself. The shrimps were huge and succulent as they were served in the Orecchiette she had also made. And the homemade antipasti and bruschetta were probably the best in all of Italy.

What a perfect dinner to talk over about the merging of two families.

Things went smoothly since no one was pregnant and it was not a forced marriage.

Gaetano was an engineering student and was almost finished with his studies. But he was not working and had to provide a dowry. That was the custom then in the area, and he had to abide by it also.

The Italian railroad was hiring and needed people to send to Northern Africa to help construct a rail system there. They were paying a cash bonus if you signed up because it was a hot desolate place and no one really wanted to live there. Gaetano thought about it and that was the only way he might pay the dowry so they could marry. That was how the three of them ended up in Northern Africa. He signed up with the understanding that after he earned an engineering degree then he would move to Northern Africa.

So they were married in a small church overlooking the bay. Everyone was happy and the wedding celebration continued well into the night.

They moved to Naples where they lived with his family for a very happy year while he continued his studies. That was where Anna Marie was born and raised until they had to move to Africa.

In the afternoons he would work in the local railroad office. He didn't do much but it paid him and also allowed him to study while working. Nobody really cared what he did; he just had to show up and punch in.

After his engineering studies were finished the railroad moved him and his family to what is now Libya.

The family packed their belongings and took their family bible with them when they walked on the ship to leave. The trip was quick and uneventful and soon they were in Northern Africa at the edge of the desert sands.

They were settled in a nice home in Tripolitania. It was in a section of the city that the other transplanted Italian emigrants decided to live, and they felt at home there and were not feeling too alone.

They could speak Italian with their neighbors, and local shopkeepers also spoke Italian and Arabic.

But the Sunni Moslem Senussi in Cyrenaica [the eastern part of Libya today] started a rebellion and things went from difficult to bad to worse for the Italians there.

There were civilian murders, political assassinations and all kinds of brutalities done by both sides. Nobody was safe.

The Italian army was sent over to quell the fighting but it just raged on and on. The rebels just fled into the desert and disappeared. It was too hot for the army and they could not maneuver as well in sand as the Berbers did. Nor were they anxious to follow them.

Eventually, all the Italians in Italian Northern Africa fled to Tripoli and tried to defend themselves in the city. But there were street killings by rebel snipers and the railroad was constantly being blown up.

Gaetano and Theresa lived in that atmosphere for a few years as their daughter grew up to be a teenager. She spoke fluently in both Italian and Arabic and played with the local kids from school.

Working in Northern Africa was extremely dangerous. Either the work could kill or maim you or the rebels would do it. It was inevitable that one or the other was going to happen if you left the safety of the city.

Anna Marie's father Gaetano was unfortunately killed one day while he was working on the outskirts of the city. He was the head engineer's assistant on the particular rail line that was being laid in the desert that day.

He and a survey crew were far ahead of the rest when they were attacked. The army had a few lightly armed soldiers with the workers but it was not enough to defend them adequately. After a brief exchange of gunfire, the soldiers were overrun and the rebels killed all the infidel workers.

The railroad had decided to try to keep laying track even though it was being blown up a week or two later. But the lead project supervisor did not care as the Italian government was paying them very handsomely to lay track and nobody from headquarters wanted to come into a war zone to inspect what was going on. So he just kept ordering track from Italy and had the men lay it in the desert. That was when the rebels attacked the work crew and shot all the men, including Gaetano.

Previously Gaetano and his family had already been living there for many years and were doing modestly well. They had adapted to the stress of war and being away from their relatives in Palermo.

Anna Marie was now a young teenager and filling out. She was starting to have a woman's body and was beginning to notice young men, and be noticed by them also.

Soon they would have to start worrying about her future.

Theresa and Gaetano had started to think that maybe they should be moving back to Palermo and their family. It was safer, and Anna Marie would have a better chance of meeting a respectable young man to marry. There were a few discussions on that subject when Theresa and Gaetano went to bed every night. It was on their minds a lot lately.

They had a small house in the city with a high walled courtyard. The home was situated in a quiet area on the southern side near the railroad station and it was decorated in the taste of the day. Nothing fancy as this was still a backwater country that time forgot.

There was sand everywhere you looked and very few paved roads if any. And if you went to the edge of the city all you saw, for as far as the eye could see were sand and more sand. It was depressing if you had grown up in the green hills of Italy.

Anna Marie and her mother decided, after Gaetano was shot and killed, to go back to Italy for safety. There was nothing there anymore to keep them in Northern Africa.

Theresa started to plan to leave Northern Africa. She purchased passage on a ship bound for Sicily and they were going to go back to Palermo.

Anna Marie was a vibrant teenager now and they had decided it was time to depart Africa and its madness.

Theresa had sold all their belongings to friends and neighbors and just took what they could carry in a suitcase or two. There was no one to purchase her home so she just left it and walked away. Gaetano had at first rented it but as he did better financially he bought it rather than moving somewhere else when their lease was up.

As usual, it was a hot day without a cloud in the sky. The sun was beating down, the dry heat was unbearable and Theresa and Anna Marie were walking to the docks when they heard gunfire.

They were on their way to the ship and were only a handful of blocks away from it when the gunfire sounded louder and closer.

Theresa was shot at and bullets pinged all around her in the dirt with wisps of sand bouncing into the air.

"Anna, they are shooting at us. I will run into the street to distract them, you must run for cover" Theresa said.

Theresa fell down in the middle of the unpaved dirt street along with other people who were really shot and some killed. She was not wounded but played dead. The bullets continued to hit the dirt street with billows of dust floating up into the air covering her with tiny mounds of dry sand.

The people who were lying in the street dared not move. Some were shot dead where they stood and some were just wounded. Their bodies lay there for almost an hour while the police and the Italian army came and started shooting back at the rebels. She was caught in a crossfire and time seemed to freeze forever. Afraid to move, Theresa yelled at Anna Marie as she fell down, to run for cover as Anna Marie was only a few steps behind her.

Desperate and only a young teenager she ran for cover into a very large building that was immediate to the left of where she was standing, and had its red front door open.

Being near the docks she did not realize that it was not a house in the typical sense, but one of ill repute. But it did not matter. The bullets were flying all over the place and it seemed safe haven from them.

When she entered and walked in it was dark with the window shades and shutters drawn shut, and had the smell of sweet incense inside. The walls were a dark stained color with some unknown brown stains running down them. Resting on large pillows scattered around the room, there were half-naked girls her age and much older, sitting and wondering what the gunshots were all about.

They were kept inside almost all the time and really had no knowledge of what was going on in the streets. The only news they heard was from either the madam or their customers. They were kept on a tight leash, almost like slaves, and a few were.

The women were a mixed group of nationalities in that bordello. There were white Italian and German girls, some blacks from central Africa, and one short Sicilian woman who seemed to be running the place. When she saw Anna Marie she thought she could use her. The wealthy men that visited her house especially liked new young white girls; especially if they were virgins.

As Anna Marie entered the building the madam ran over to Anna Marie and slapped her in the face, startling her. Anna Marie just froze for a moment from the shock of the blow. Then the madam went to grab Anna Marie by the hair and pull her into a back room to begin her obedience training that afternoon. This woman had no morals and saw a valuable gift running in the door. She was smiling at the thought of the money this girl would bring in, and her yellow teeth with their gaps in the front made a slight whistling sound as she would breadth through her mouth.

The madam kept the names of some wealthy local businessmen and sheiks that had visited her before the rebellion started. They had mentioned they wanted to increase their harems. They lived in tents in the desert and rarely came into the city. Anna Marie would be a big money maker once they came and they saw her. The madam could decide later if she wanted to sell her or just keep her working in her bordello. She felt there was no rush to decide right away on Anna Marie's future.

She yelled at the black girl "open the door to the back room and get the lock. I don't want her to escape. She is worth a lot of money."

But the madam's left hand slipped down over Anna Marie's face and it stopped in front of her mouth. Anna Marie bit down hard on a finger that was near her front teeth. The madam released her grip on her for just a moment, but that was all the time she needed to escape.

Anna Marie dashed out the red door with all her strength just at the moment when the madam released her. Yelling curse words at Anna Marie, and in great pain, the madam started to chase her out into the street. She did not want this prize to escape.

They were still shooting outside but Anna Marie, in her excitement to escape, never heard the gunshots. She ran with all her might down the side of the street towards the ship and was able to get almost to the gangplank when she realized that she had to take cover.

They were shooting at her now and she finally realized that she was a target. The dust pings were hitting the ground all around her. She dove behind a stack of wooden crates that were ready to be loaded upon the ship. Her face was wet from sweat and it stuck to the coarse wood of the crates as she rested her head against the warm wood. When she moved her head away from the crate there were small splinters of wood stuck to her.

She was safe there so she did not move from behind them until she saw the Italian soldiers in their desert uniforms passing by in front of her, and her mother came running to get her.

The madam did run out the red door and into the street after her but when they started to shoot directly at her she realized what was going on and turned around and quickly ran back inside to safety.

After a few minutes that seemed like hours Anna Marie heard the gunshots stop and people started to come out and walk on the street again. Miraculously her mother was not injured and was able to get up and run to the dock to reunite with Anna Marie.

They both were able to board the ship, without their suitcases, and were taken to Palermo. They left their bags on the street behind them. They were afraid to go back to get them. It was too dangerous and they did not want to leave the ship.

Theresa had arranged beforehand with the boarding agent their departure and had sewn the tickets into her dress so as not to lose them. Luckily for her, she did that.

Their passage was already paid for and they boarded the ship with just the clothes they were wearing.

Both of them did not know they were the only women on the ship until the first mate told them to stay in their rooms and he will bring them food and water.

It was not safe for them to come up to the deck while the men were working. Only at night were they to come up and see the water and breathe fresh air.

That night there was a knock on their stateroom door asking if they wanted some wine. Theresa did not recognize the voice and declined. She was not about to open the door unless it was the first mate. They had decided on a password so she would know it was him.

Years before the first mate had studied for the priesthood but eventually did not feel he had a calling for it. He had met a young woman in the church and he left before taking his final vows. This was the only job that he could get so he set off on this ship. But he still had a feeling for humanity and knew right from wrong.

It was not a long journey, about two days, and they soon arrived at Palermo, Sicily.

Theresa's family had come from there and she knew she would be able to find work in a café.

After arriving in Palermo they settled in with Theresa's cousin and arrangements were made for them to live in one room above a nearby store.

Anna Marie is hired working in a local bakery for very long hours and her mother started to look for work during the day.

Theresa was walking down the Via Trapani with the midday sun beating down on her. It was getting hotter as the day went on and there was no breeze that day coming in off the sea.

She was getting tired looking for work when she saw this small café with a help wanted a sign in the window.

It was the usual type of small café with tables outside, bentwood chairs to sit on and a striped awning unfurled half way down. The aroma of coffee floated in the air and there were a few people sitting outside eating and talking. Inside was a small bar that served liquor. It was not far from the waterfront and many people were walking about the street.

Needing a job she walked in and asked a waitress, who turned out to be the owner's wife that she would like to see the proprietor. He was an older man working behind a small wooden bar where he served wine and took care of the cash box.

There were three fans slowly circulating the warm air inside giving off just enough of a breeze that one could feel it if they were motionless.

No one was wearing a jacket and the sweat stains on everyone's shirts said enough about the weather.

Theresa told the owner she would like to work as a waitress and that she spoke two languages, Italian of course and a little Arabic from her years in Northern Africa. He liked that and saw a spunky side while talking to her so she was hired. She looked like an energetic person and he had had enough lazy workers in the past.

Theresa had to come in the next day very early and was shown around the kitchen and bar. She was given instructions on how much they charged and where everything was to be placed on the tables. She picked it up very quickly.

She worked long hours in the café; from noon till the early hours of the morning. Serving during the day and night and cleaning up after everyone had left she made herself necessary to the running of the café. And the owner, who was an older man, took notice and appreciated her industriousness.

Theresa usually wore a lightly colored cotton dress with small flowers on it that she had sewn herself. It hung loosely over her small frame and swayed when she walked. She had a lot of very similar dresses, as she had made them all on an old sewing machine to save money. But she did look very striking in them and men noticed her.

It was there she met a handsome young man who had taken a liking to her. But the feelings were not mutual.

He had an attitude about himself that did not sit well with Theresa's fiery personality. She was not about to let this peacock rule over her. She was too independent for that to happen.

Although he was dressed in the fashion of the day and his thick wavy hair played well against his good looks; she would have none of him. His condescending attitude towards her ticked her off. She was courteous to him, but not enamored of him.

After a few nights of serving him with the local dry red wine he preferred and rebuffing his advances, he decided to leave the café early. He waited down the block for the café to close and he started to follow her for a few blocks when she left. She did not notice that he was walking slowly and discretely behind her.

When she turned and started to walk down a darkened street he ran after her and caught her from behind.

He put a knife to her throat and pulled her into an alley. He had grabbed her by the hair and pushed her body forcefully into the brick wall of the building. It knocked her breath away, her eyes turned upward in a daze, she immediately felt weak and her legs started to give out from under her.

To continue to hold her up he quickly thrust his hand between her legs and started to roughly rub her genitals. He let go of her neck and with a vengeful tearing, he tore at her thin cotton dress until it ripped off of her thin petite body. Then he threw her down onto the cold damp ground like a piece of garbage.

He looked at her in a most lecherous way.

"Don't even think to scream or I will cut your throat. When I want a whore like you I will take her. Nobody refuses me" he said.

When she heard that she stopped resisting him and vowed to herself to take her revenge someday. She knew what was coming and resigned herself to the inevitable. "I will survive this" she silently thought to herself.

He raped her repeatedly. Finally, when finished he stood and looked at her in disgust lying on the ground with tears silently streaming down her face. He felt no remorse. She was just another helpless girl he abused. And she knew it. Spitting out the words in conquest and contempt, he bent over her and said: "maybe now you will remember me and not refuse me next time".

He turned and walked out of the alley without even glancing back at her.

She knew who he was and knew better than to report it to the police. He was the son of a local Don and was not to be fooled with. With just a word to his father, her whole family would be killed. But he did not know who she was, just that he wanted to have sex with her on a whim.

When he finally left after he was finished leering at her naked body, and her being totally exposed lying helplessly on the floor of the alley she with great effort is able to stand. She was in pain and her head hurt due to him also slamming her to the floor of the alley. Bleeding from a forceful rape, and wobbly, she started to lean against the brick wall for support as she stood up. She did not stop shedding tears from the humiliation of being raped, but from knowing that this was not the end of it. Her honor was at stake, and she would revenge her dishonor somehow.

Theresa picked up her clothes from the street and tried to hold together her torn and ripped cotton dress over her as best she could. It was in the early hours of the morning and luckily no one was out strolling on the streets.

The sun did not come up yet as she walked quickly home hoping no one would see her. Being close to the water the mist from the sea wafted in and helped cover her escape to safety. She could smell the salt in the air as she scrambled home. She had no thoughts except to get home to Anna Marie and safety.

Theresa knew she had to get out of the country or this would happen again whenever he felt like it.

She was an unknown girl in a big city, and he was the godfather's son.

Theresa was at his mercy now. She felt depressed and feared for her daughter's and her safety if she refused him in the future. She had no choice but to tell her family what had happened to her that night and how she was disrespected. Her parents were dead and she had only her uncle and cousins.

Sicily, like the rest of Italy, was no picnic at that time.

Mussolini had come to power and things were not great. Theresa's relatives felt sorry for her and Anna Marie and did not want extra mouths to feed and care for if she did not go back to work. Times were tough.

The family met one night and decided that arrangements for Theresa and Anna Marie to go to America had to be made. They knew of the Don and did not want to get revenge fearing for their own family's safety and well-being.

The Italian railroad paid for the tickets after Theresa's cousins quietly met with the railroad agent one evening to discuss the matter. After a brief discussion between the agent and her three cousins, the agent decided the railroad had to buy the boarding passes for them because Gaetano was killed while working for the railroad in Libya. At least that is what Theresa's family told her before she left.

In reality, the family felt terrible they would not be able to protect them from the Don's son; so they spoke to the agent in a way he could not refuse.

Two tickets to New York were obtained and they were to leave in two weeks after that for America.

Hearing the news that night from her uncle that he and his sons had arranged for her to go to America, Theresa knew what she had to do.

Her honor was stolen from her by that rape and she did not want to involve her cousins in her revenge. The Don's son did not know who she was or where she lived. He did not follow her home long enough that night to find out.

The evening before they were to leave Theresa again worked at the café and waited for her rapist to come in and order. HE was there very often and she knew his schedule. This was her first time back at work since the being raped.

Theresa was very charming and jovial that night. When the rapist sat down she approached him, smiled, and quietly said to him that she changed her mind and would like to be with him again.

"Tonight when the cafe closes come back and I would like to be with you," Theresa whispered in his ear as she leaned over to serve him a coffee.

She said she liked it when he took control. He smiled. Tonight will be an easier conquest he thought to himself.

They had arranged to meet before the café shut down for the evening and he would stay there with her while she cleaned up.

When the café was almost closed and the lights were out, he stayed and waved to the owner that he would close up for him. Knowing who he was the proprietor knew he should not argue with him, and he left. This had happened before and he was not concerned. Only Theresa and her rapist were alone in the darkened café.

49

He slowly walked over to her. The lighting was soft; some would call it dim, some dark. He told her "I am glad you came to your senses, and I will be gentler this time".

She was standing by the bar holding a rag and lightly dusting, wiping the top of the bar, smiling at him. "I am sorry I refused you before," Theresa said. "I should not have been so aristocratic" she murmured.

Theresa was waiting for him to come closer to her. She had unbuttoned the top two buttons on her dress.

He anticipated an easier night of pleasure.

As he approached, coming almost nose-to-nose with her, Theresa grabbed the sharpened knife that she was holding under the rag and lunged at his throat. She was not a large woman, actually very petite, but with all her rage and might she swung at his throat and cut it just right. As the sharpened blade entered she twisted it back and forth, side to side, and almost took his head off.

"Let's see how manly you are now, you are squealing like a stuck pig," Theresa shouted out to him as he grabbed at his neck.

He fell to the ground gurgling and gasping for breath, spewing blood all over the floor. He was thrashing about, kicking the chairs and tables in a grotesque dance of death.

Theresa stood her ground looking at him as he helplessly was swirling about.

Finally, he stopped moving. His body relaxed and fell limp before her eyes. Her rapist was dead.

She bent down close to his body and cut his pants off by his crotch. Then she grabbed his manhood, cut it off, and threw it down beside his head. Quickly she stood to leave and locked the door behind her, never looking back as he had done to her.

Her honor was restored.

She walked briskly to her room over the store where she was staying with her daughter.

Theresa quickly woke Anna Marie and told her to get dressed. Then she grabbed the suitcases that they had already packed the day before and they both hurried to the docks to get on the ship for America. Unlike Northern Africa, nobody was shooting at them…yet.

Theresa had the tickets her uncles had given her clutched in her hand.

They both excitedly ran down the stairway to the street and started to walk at a quick pace to the docks. She was looking for the ship that would carry them to America and a future.

As they approached the docks they saw it. There was a huge ship tied to the dock being filled with cargo bound for New York. Its hold was filled with olive oil, dried figs, sun-dried tomatoes and crates of white and red Italian wines. It was much bigger than the one she took from North Africa; this was a ship that could traverse the oceans of the world.

She and Anna Marie walked hastily up the gangplank of the freighter and boarded as quickly as they could while the cargo was still being loaded.

They were taken to a small inner cabin below deck. They both stayed in the room until the ship left port slightly before dawn.

***

The next day when the shopkeeper opened up his café for business he saw the body on the floor in a huge pool of blood. He noticed the genitals lying on the ground next to his head. Immediately he called the police and the police chief, after a brief investigation, in a whisper announced to the proprietor that it was an apparent murder by an unknown person.

Knowing whom the victim was he and the proprietor decided that one troublemaker had met a just ending. And if he really said what he was thinking there would be more killings to revenge his death. Why start something where innocent people might get killed, he thought to himself. He was not a fan of the Don, although he was indebted to him for some favors in the past. But this time justice was done.

The shopkeeper had decided that he would not tell the police that he knew who the girl was that stayed with the godfather's son the night before.

He did say to the police it was some whore that he never saw before if they had asked him in depth about who might have done this. That was believable because they all knew the son's reputation with the women of the evening. He would frequently troll the streets around the docks late at night looking for prostitutes. Otherwise, the proprietor would be caught between the godfather and Theresa's family. Let the police say it was a whore, and he would be safely out of the picture.

It was not unusual for the shopkeeper to let the Don's son stay after hours. He had done it many times before as he even had a key to the cafe.

***

There was a wealthy cousin that Theresa was told to see when she arrived in New York. The family in Palermo thought that all people in America were wealthy. The streets thought to be paved with gold and silver.

But the cousins were not wealthy but very hard working people who barely made a living working in the city.

When the ship arrived in New York Harbor they were taken to Ellis Island where they were medically checked and then admitted to America. Their cousins from Brooklyn came to escort them away from the island and to the ferry to Manhattan. Then they had to take the ferry from Manhattan to Brooklyn and a trolley ride home from the Red Hook docks.

After they made their way to Bensonhurst and the cousin's home they were shown a small bedroom that would be theirs for the immediate future.

That night at dinner the cousins started to tell them about Brooklyn and Manhattan [the city]. They were told where they might find work and how to go about getting a job.

The next day they all walked around Bensonhurst showing them the stores and where to shop. But they had to find work quickly so they could be settled somewhere permanently on their own.

Eventually, through the local church, a priest referred them to a clothing factory in Manhattan where they both found work sewing. There they were employed doing piecework in a sweatshop in the garment district in midtown. The hours were long and the working conditions not so great.

They were working alongside Jews, Italians, and Greeks; all working peacefully. No one understood the language that the others were speaking but they were able to get by. In broken English and sign language, they all coexisted peacefully.

The union boss came to visit often and speak to them about joining. But he had to wait downstairs outside the building. He was not allowed in to talk to them while they were working. If they walked out and spoke to the organizer and the foreman saw them, they would be fired. It was very stressful for new immigrants.

When they left for the day the organizer would hand them flyers about what the union could do for them. But it was in English and Theresa and Anna Marie only spoke Italian and Arabic. But it did not matter. They were not joining anything right now. They were happy to have a roof over their heads and money to buy food.

Both Anna Marie and her mother had started to work together in the same clothing factory.

Her mother, Theresa, stayed there for years at the same factory, but Anna Marie had started looking for another job. She did not like the factory owner and thought he was creepy with his slicked back hair and tiny pencil line mustache.

He spoke both Italian and English and ran a very tight workplace. There was no slacking off. Just work, and when he walked through the plant he would always stop by Theresa's sewing machine to see if it was working correctly. He had his eye on her for things other than work.

When he was near Anna Marie he would sometimes just stand there and stare at her, visually undressing her with his eyes. This unnerved her and she felt that something was going to happen to her so she decided to leave.

Besides he was much older than her and she did not think he was good looking.

But Theresa for some reason is able to get along with him, and they started to date.

Maybe it was the security of his money that she liked? Who knows why people get together? After many years of living hand to mouth, who cannot understand the reasons that people do things?

He always treated her with respect feeling that she was not a person to be fooled with. She was very good looking and petite but had an attitude that you immediately knew where you stood with her. Just one frosty look from her steely eyes and you knew where you stood.

Theresa never married again but dated him for many years until he died.

He took very good care of her financially and helped her to settle down in America. She started to have a more comfortable lifestyle by dating him.

When he died he left her some money, two buildings, and some jewelry that she quickly put under her mattress. She did not trust the banks. Theresa was not the same innocent girl that Gaetano had married. Life had hardened her.

She would not even think to remarry, not him or anyone else. The memory of her love for Gaetano was still in her heart and in her mind. That was her first and truest love. Nobody ever knew if she ever really loved the factory owner, but she was kind to him and he on his part treated her with respect and love.

Anna Marie soon left that factory where her mother worked. She started another sewing job in a handmade custom tailor shop just around the corner from her mother's factory. The tailor had a small retail store in the garment center of Manhattan where he sold and fitted his wealthy customers.

They both continued to live with their cousins in Brooklyn for a little while longer. They stayed in a furnished room in the basement of their home and used to commute to the city together in the mornings.

After dating the factory owner for a while he decided that he would rent an apartment for Theresa and Anna Marie to live in. It was near a train station so they would not have far to walk to get to work. He paid the rent for them, and Theresa continued to see him "socially" because she wanted to.

Anna Marie was not stupid, just not formally educated like they do for children in America. In Europe, most girls were not sent to school. They were taught to cook and sew and eventually be mothers and wives.

She was smart enough to eventually marry someone who was gainfully employed and raise a family.

Anna Marie's immediate manager in the tailor shop thought she was attractive and tried to date her. He had asked her out to go to dinner with him after work.

"Anna Marie, if you are not busy tonight after work would you like to go for dinner with me?"

He spoke fluent Italian but he was married and she would not go out with a married man. Her mother had warned her of such things happening when they were in Palermo, and she did not forget her lessons.

Frustrated with not being able to meet with her the manager decided that he would introduce her to a cousin of his. He thought that maybe once she married she might be more inclined to eventually have a romance with him. He had bedded many married women before and thought this might be the way to get in bed also. So one day he introduced her to his cousin Mario.

Mario was a nice young man who worked delivering furniture for Macy's. He drove a truck all over the city bringing new furniture into people's homes, and he made a nice living. It was hard honest work but he did not mind. The money was decent and the tips were excellent.

He was a very muscular man and especially even-tempered. When he was introduced to Anna Marie he took an immediate liking to her.

They dated for a short while and then they decided they would get married.

Mario came one evening to pick up Anna Marie and he brought flowers for Theresa.

"Theresa, these flowers are for you. I am in love with Anna Marie and would like your permission to marry her."

Theresa knew he was a good decent man, and she approved. They were married soon after in a small church wedding in Bensonhurst.

Anna Marie continued to work until her husband died many years later. She stayed home after that and lived frugally on Mario's social security and his union pension from Macy's.

The years had passed since their wedding and Anna Marie never cheated on her husband, and never slept with another man while he was alive, or even after he died.

After the marriage, Mario and Anna Marie looked for a house to buy and they found one in Bensonhurst near 78th street. It was a two family brick home and they moved in. Theresa helped them with the down payment from some of the money she was given by the factory owner.

They took the rooms upstairs.

Mario, with only kindness in his heart, asked Theresa to move in also. And she lived with them in their walk-in street-level apartment downstairs. It had an entrance by the driveway so she did not have to climb stairs.

She moved out of her apartment in Manhattan that the factory owner had rented for her. But he often visited with her overnight in Brooklyn.

This is a common type of household arrangement in that area of Brooklyn. It was built as a two family home so parents could live with their married daughter. It is called a mother-daughter home.

Anna Marie, after a few the years of marriage, had three daughters with Mario. They were Gina Marie, Mary Catherine, and Carmen.

Chapter 4 –

Gina Marie was not always this size.

As a teenager, she was not a slim girl but built solidly with curves, and she turned heads when she walked down 86th street. The black girls in the city use the word "thick" to describe that look. Not fat, just thick.

Her highly teased hair framed her face and she only wore tight clothes except when she was in school. The parochial schools required uniforms and the girl's skirts had to come down to below their knees. But Gina Marie and her friends always rolled up their skirts by their waists. This brought the skirt up above their knees. They did this every day just before the end of school when they left to walk home. This attracted the boy's attention from the nearby boy's parochial school.

She was not a sophisticated girl in any way. Gina Marie took everyone at their face value and she believed what was told to her if it made any kind of sense.

The best way to describe her would be that she was a follower and did not see below the surface on anything.

Only a few blocks away a boy's parochial school was located, and the two school's students would mingle on a street corner away from the nun's prying eyes before going home. It started as innocent flirting in the younger grades, and as they matured dates would be made, and relationships started.

The middle-aged school women who worked part-time as crossing guards usually had to break up the crowds and shoo them home and away from the corner so other people could pass.

Local churches usually held formal dances for the kids to meet each other under the supervision of the nuns and priests. But the boys usually didn't dance, or even go to them unless their mothers actually walked them there.

What could you do with nuns watching that you don't dance too close to one another? That was no fun. But they would find a way to sneak out a side door and a few of them would make out in the darkness of the schoolyard with only the street lights watching them.

The street corner was the usual hangout. There were many corners to meet someone and if they were on a date they would often end up at Jan's on 86th street for ice cream or a burger.

Jan's was famous for what it called "The Kitchen Sink". It was a large bowl of ice cream piled high that could feed half of New York City. The young men always tried to see who could eat one completely. But it was also a good way to share with a date and have some laughs.

That was how Gina met Rocco, on a street corner, at Bay Parkway and 86th Street, while she was waiting for a bus standing in front of the Chock Full O'Nuts coffee shop. She had just gone in and bought a hot chocolate to keep warm while she waited outside, leaning against the window trying to protect herself from the slight breeze coming down the avenue from the bay.

It was a sunny Saturday afternoon in the fall and the buses were running on a weekend schedule. That means very few of them, and far between.

It is standard practice for New York City bus drivers to be told by their supervisors that there are a million reasons why you can be behind schedule, but none for being early. So why rush?

Rocco noticed her standing there and walked over to Gina Marie and asked: "do youse have da time?" That was his pickup line. It was lame, but it seemed to have worked in the past.

"Yer, its tree o'clock. What's yer name" she answered.

She thought he was cute.

"Rocco, do youse mind if I wait here wit youse"?

"Naw, ya can keep me comp'ny" she answered him. "My name's Gina Marie".

She was very striking with her full curvaceous body tightly bound in a white frilly blouse stretching in the front at the buttons, and skin tight blue jeans.

Rocco was on the heavy muscular side with thick curly black hair combed back, then the front pushed forward. His most striking feature was a protruding Roman nose set in the middle of a round pockmarked face. He was not bad looking but when he stared at you, with a serious face, he was menacing to look at.

He then told her "youse are very cute. How bout see'in a movie wit me nex Sat'day night?" There was a moment of silence. "Ya know" he continued, "youse would have a good time an it's ah Tab Hunter movie".

That seemed to do it and she accepted his offer; "Okay I'll go wit youse to see dat movie". She gave him her phone number on a piece of paper she took out of her pocketbook and scribbled on it her mother's home phone.

"Now remember ta call me afta seven clock cause I have ta do homework," she told him.

There was no guarantee he would call, but he asked for her phone number and she believed he would call. And he did.

Being forward is normal in this neighborhood, especially for the young men.

Rocco had graduated from New Utrecht High School the previous June and was just hanging around doing odd jobs here and there. He had no job skills and was not seriously looking for work either.

His father was a sanitation worker for the city and his mother worked in a local children's shoe store on Avenue N near McDonald Avenue. The overtime his dad made kept the family living a comfortable lifestyle.

Some of the other guys didn't want to work that much but Rocco's dad always asked for overtime and his supervisor made sure he received it. The supervisor always would get a kickback at the end of the month for arranging the extra overtime work. It was nothing too much, but enough to keep everyone happy. That is how things work in the sanitation department.

They would pull out of the garage at five in the morning, stop for breakfast at seven, and then finish their day and be back in the garage by one in the afternoon after they stopped for lunch at eleven.

If they put in four hours of work a day they considered it a full day. There was no one to say differently. Their supervisors all came up through the ranks and did the same thing when they were on the trucks working the routes. And they knew the guys because the chances were they had worked with them at some point in time, and they all socialized together also.

***

One of the older neighborhood guys that lived down the block from Rocco, named Paulie, often saw him hanging around and suggested to Rocco that he get his driver's license. Paulie told him he needed someone to drive him to his businesses throughout the city, and it was easy money.

Paulie always wore a suit or sports jacket but never was too flashy. His gray hair and clean-shaven face did not draw the attention away from a large jagged scar he had under his left ear. It ran from his ear down to his collarbone. It was the result of a fight he was in as a young man on the lower east side of Manhattan. But his opponent faired much worse than he did.

That fight resulted in his elevation and eventually to a leadership role in the mob.

Rocco had no future aspirations or job prospects, so he took his driver's license test, past it, and accepted the job offer from Paulie.

Of course, Rocco practiced driving Paulie around before he actually received his license. He never bothered with the technicalities that the law required. He felt they didn't apply to him.

Often he would drive him on Bay Parkway or under McDonald Avenue to his favorite Italian restaurant near Avenue U. He practiced driving, and never hit anything or anyone, unintentionally.

The money was good. He was paid in cash and all he had to do was drive Paulie to his business locations, and keep his mouth shut on what he saw and heard. He was getting big bucks chauffeuring him around and Rocco knew his place in the scheme of things.

Then late one afternoon he was asked to drive Paulie and Paulie's friend Sal to a downtown Manhattan address.

"Hey, Paulie," Rocco asked, "Ya have ta tell me how to get deer. I nev'ah drove to duh city ba'for".

"No problem" Sal answered him. "Jus head for the Will-ims-burg Bridge an I'll tell ya where ta turn. Its get'in late and we might hit duh rush hour traffic on duh Belt."

There was a lot of stop and go traffic leading to the Williamsburg Bridge and they didn't get to Manhattan until it was almost dark outside.

"Go straight on ta Houston" Sal told him. "Then make ah turn on ta Sixth Aven-new and go uptown a bit". After a short while Rocco turned onto a cross street and then onto Seventh Avenue.

Rocco had never driven in traffic like this before. Paulie had him driving in Brooklyn and Queens and sometimes over the Verrazano Bridge to Staten Island. But this was his first time in the city. He was not used to such heavy congestion. Driving past parked trucks on the narrow side streets made squeezing by a new skill. But Rocco took his time and managed to get by without hitting anything.

Paulie told him "don't stop in the middle of an intersection. You'll get a ticket and I don't want ta pay it." So he was very careful about watching the red lights and drove extra carefully. Paulie did not want to get stopped that night.

When they arrived at the address on Seventh Avenue Sal told him to stop the car in front of a pizza place. "Deer it is" he said. Dis is where we'z goin. Jus stop an let us out" Sal said. Rocco was double-parked in rush hour traffic and was causing a major backup in a very short time.

Paulie and Sal exited the car and went into a pizza parlor.

"Circle round da block ah couple times till I come and tell ya ta stop" Sal yelled at Rocco above the noise of the cars, with their horns blasting.

Rocco drove around the block for about thirty minutes or so until Sal came out and waved at him to stop.

"Double park, open duh trunk, and help me carry some'tin out to duh car" Sal yelled at Rocco with his low musky voice, again trying to be heard above the clatter of traffic.

When Rocco went into the pizza parlor he saw the tables were thrown around and there was a large burlap bag tied tight sitting in the middle of the floor.

There was nobody else in the place except for Paulie.

"Pick dis up wit me an let's get duh hell out'a here," Sal told Rocco in a matter of fact voice.

Rocco grabbed the top of the burlap bag where it was tied tight and helped lift it and bring it outside to the double-parked car. They both strained to pick it up and throw the heavy bag into the open car trunk. They heaved it with all their strength, and it landed with a loud thump. Paulie slammed the trunk shut once it fell in.

Rocco thought he heard some moans coming out of the bag but they were muffled and he knew better than to ask questions.

Then Rocco ran around to the driver's side, hopped in, and they all drove away.

Paulie told Rocco "drive to Staten Island and den to Jersey. We're go-in to Lantic City tonight.

Rocco wasn't sure how to get there but he knew that the Staten Island Expressway went to Staten Island and to a bridge into New Jersey. He never had any reason to go to Jersey before, so he didn't.

He had heard of the Jersey Shore and the beaches, but he either went to Coney Island or Brighton Beach in the summer.

Rocco preferred Brighton Beach because of the Lincoln Savings Bank on the corner of Coney Island Avenue and Brighton Beach Avenue.

Some Russian kid from high school had told Rocco what his cousin and aunt did when they went to the beach there, and he thought that was a great idea, so he did it too. They would rent a small safety deposit box in the basement of the bank for five dollars a year. When the bank opened at nine in the morning they would go down, take out the safety deposit box and in the private room by the vault they would change into their swim trunks. As long as they were back to the bank before three o'clock they could change again and leave in dry clothes. They had discovered that for only five dollars a year they could use the vault at the bank as a cabana. The real cabanas at the beach went for thousands a year if there was even one available.

He drove to Canal Street and took the bridge over to Brooklyn following the signs that would lead him to Staten Island.

Rocco kept driving until he crossed the Outer bridge Crossing over the Kill Van Kull to route 440 and was told to continue to the Garden State Parkway south.

"Jus keep drive-in," Sal told him. "I'll tell ya when ta get off duh highway."

He drove past the Black Horse Turnpike and turned off at the next exit. Sal told him to drive in a westerly direction. After driving a while Paulie told him to turn onto a dirt road. The only light was from their car headlights and it was a very bumpy trail, not even a road. Finally, after a half hour on this dirt trail, they stopped alongside some pine trees and tall grass, next to an open field. They were in the middle of nowhere. It was pitch black and only their headlights enabled them to see anything on the ground. But the stars were bright, and Rocco looked up and noticed them when he stepped out of the car.

A few years before, Paulie had bought the property with the intention of building a summer house away from the city. But New Jersey's Governor Byrne had put a moratorium on building in the Pine Barrens so he was stuck with land that he could not build on. But he found another use for it, though.

Sal opened the trunk and gave Rocco a shovel. "Here, take a shovel and start digging," Sal told him in Italian. The two of them started to dig in the soft earth. They were digging a grave.

It wasn't too deep because it was late, they were tired, and wanted to get on with it.

"Hey Paulie", Sal asked, "Maybe we can go to Lantic City after this. I know a good bar and whore house there"?

Paulie didn't answer.

"Its deep enough now, let's gets the bag from the car," Sal said to Rocco.

Sal and Rocco grabbed the burlap bag to lift it out of the trunk. Rocco smelled cologne coming through the burlap. The sweet smell of cologne mixing in the air with the aroma of the pine trees made Rocco feel queasy.

His senses were on overload, and his legs were a little wobbly from nerves, but Rocco never lets on. He knew what they were doing, even though they never said a word to him about anything. He never experienced anything like this before.

"You did a good job tonight kid," Paulie said. "Here, take this gun and shoot it at the bag a few times."

He did this to test Rocco, and ensure that he would keep his mouth shut. Rocco realized that if he didn't shoot into the bag, he could be the next one in the grave.

Rocco did it and was now "involved". He had pointed the gun at the bag and pulled the trigger a few times. The bag jumped with each shot and then there was no movement. The gunshots rang out in the black night air but they were the only ones who heard it.

This was Paulie's way of testing him, and also ensuring his silence.

Sal and Rocco then lifted the bag and dumped it into the hole. They started to cover it with the dirt they previously dug up. Finally, when it was covered they put some tree branches over it, and nobody would ever suspect a thing. It blended in with the area.

Paulie put his hand into his left pants pocket and pulled out a few hundred dollar bills, and hand them to Rocco. "Here," he said proudly, "you did good."

This was big money, and it sealed the deal for Rocco. He became Paulie's official driver, and one of his enforcers.

All three of them sat back in the car and headed for Atlantic City.

Paulie did a few favors in Manhattan for a guy he knew from Philly, Arturo Romano, and he owed him a good time. So tonight he was going to collect on the favor.

Rocco drove over the bridge on the Black Horse Pike and into Atlantic City. He then turned right and headed for the area near the airport.

There was a large house on a back road that had a long driveway behind some small piney woods. Rocco drove up to the house and parked on the side, near some bushes.

They all opened the doors and walked out of the car over to the wooden wrap around porch. The only light was coming from side windows that were on each side of the front door. The three of them stood there for a moment looking for the bell. But there was none. There was no need for one. The door opened almost immediately and they were ushered inside.

An older Italian woman on the small side, with a full head of white hair, pulled back, greeted them. Although she was on the small side she had huge pointy breasts, a tight gold dress on, and was told by someone from Philly to probably expect them to visit her. She escorted the three of them into a small first-floor parlor and selected a top-shelf whiskey for Paulie from a small bar that was there. Sal and Rocco each had a cold beer.

Five women walked in and Paulie selected first and walked upstairs with her. She was a light-skinned Dominican girl, almost white.

Rocco and Sal then selected their dates and went in the back of the house to the bedrooms there. Sal chose a tall, thick, black girl with jerry curls and they left the parlor arm in arm. Rocco liked dark-skinned Spanish girls and he had his choice of the remaining two. One was a white skinned, very fat, a heavy set blond named Bobbie from Jersey, and the other was a darker girl. So he took both sluts by their hand and they walked into the back to a waiting bedroom.

Bobbie was almost never picked unless she was the last one, or there was a fatty lover coming to the house. As a young girl, she was always in fights at school over her weight and name-calling. She wasn't stupid, just fat and ugly too.

It was in the wee hours of the morning before they finally were all finished.

After two hours in the bedrooms, they all met in the parlor again and left for Brooklyn.

They thanked their dates and Paulie gave them all a very big tip.

Before he left Paulie whispered to the madam to please thank his host from Philly for the evening. He appreciated his generosity.

Paulie and Sal slept in the car for the whole ride back. Luckily Rocco didn't drink a lot, and kind of remembered how to get home.

And the Parkway's rest stop coffee also helped keep him awake.

***

After that night Rocco started to dress better but kept odd hours.

The pizza parlors Paulie visited were fronts for illegal drug distribution, prostitution, gambling and other businesses Paulie owned or controlled.

Each week Paulie would stop in to collect his share. Now that Rocco was with him he would sometimes send him in to collect the money while he stayed in the car. Especially if it was raining or snowing he would not go out. Rocco was trusted and in training.

Each place had a different percentage take.

If there was a shortage Rocco was told to do what he had to in order to collect. Sal had spoken to him and gave him some instructions on collecting from people.

Rocco rarely had to use violence. Usually, a stern look and a mild threat were enough. "Youse never knows where lightning is gonna strike" he would tell them. They understood what he was saying. "Build-ins could catch fire if lightning hit dem" he would often tell the people who did not catch on immediately and pay. Or "a car can splode if it wuz hit". That usually was the clincher.

Sometimes he would only have to place his hand on the guy's arm and gently squeeze it to get his message across. He always walked out with the money.

If it was a woman who was trying to hold out he would tell them "Deer are op'nings in a whore house in Harlem that could use someone like youse".

They always paid. Just the thought of what could happen was enough, and the money was always brought forth. They knew the people they were dealing with, were not going to screw with them, and live to tell about it.

Early in his collecting career, he had to convince someone that he couldn't steal from Paulie and get away with it. Rocco took the guy by the arm and placed his hand into the open pizza oven onto the hot bricks. That was enough to give Rocco a reputation. He never had to do it again.

Paulie was also involved in prostitution. He helped finance a few brothels for madams who gladly paid him back in cash and product. They were all over Queens, Brooklyn and a few downtown in the financial district of Manhattan. They all made really big money.

The stockbrokers who worked in the area would visit, drop big bucks, and always take clients for a special thank you for your business. The brothels in lower Manhattan were all located in office buildings on top floors so it appeared that the men were there on business when they entered the building lobby.

One brothel that Paulie owned in the city was located in the basement of an apartment house in mid-town Manhattan. When you drove into the underground public parking garage the valet took your car. If you asked for apartment 27B, he would point you to a steel door at the rear of the garage behind an extremely large column that hid it from sight.

When you rang the bell on the steel door you had to wait for someone to look at you through a remote camera. Then you had to ask if this was apartment 27B. Only then were you let in. Once you were admitted you never saw anything like this before. They had a pool, a bar, and plenty of attractive young nude women swimming or walking around for your pleasure. It was Sodom and Gomorrah reincarnated in the middle of Manhattan. Of course, there were private rooms available also for those men who wanted to be discrete.

It was a very high-class operation and ornately decorated. The colors were burgundy and gold with lots of brass everywhere. Many businessmen and salesmen used it like frequent flyer miles for their clients. Buy enough, you'll get enough points, and then get admitted to the basement brothel.

One lady Paulie knew, "Big Sally," he helped to finance a high-end brothel on 86th street in Brooklyn; just above Bucky Baccatelli's 24-hour candy store. In the neighborhood, it was just known as Bucky's and was a favorite place for the kids to stop in and buy candy or fountain sodas. Bucky himself worked there and would mix the syrup and seltzer right in front of you into a glass. Five cents bought you a small glass, ten cents for a larger one. In the summer months, Bucky sold a lot of large sodas.

His most popular drink was a "Lime Ricky" and he sold a lot of them during the warm weather. It was basically a mix of cherry syrup and seltzer, and then he would add in lime juice. There is no better word to describe it in the summer than fabulously delicious and refreshing.

***

Big Sally was a plus size woman, and she took no crap from anyone. Her whores knew better than to start with her, and clients were treated with the respect she demanded they be given. The two bouncers she employed as bartenders also insured a quiet demeanor. This brothel eventually became Rocco's home away from home.

She had started in a small one family house in the Midwood section of Brooklyn between Avenue's M and N on a small cross street. Her home was on a corner with a side entrance. When you parked your car across the street from her, and she heard your car door close she would peer out the window to see if you were coming to her place. If she was not greeting her guests she was always by the window.

The brothel usually opened about five o'clock in the afternoon, and if you walked by you could see the four or five girls standing outside waiting for her to open the door. They were a mixed group. Some black, some white, some Spanish, and she even had a black transvestite for those who requested it.

The new one on 86th street was different.

You walked into a twenty-four-hour candy store and went to the back wall. After paying $50 for candy, you then were admitted into a very elegant hall/lobby and through a solid wrought iron door with baroque filigree on it.

There was a very plush carpeted staircase that led upstairs where the brothel was expensively furnished and extremely upscale. You could see that a lot of money was spent fixing it up. This brothel took up the two floors above the candy store and faced the elevated train. The windows were curtained and slightly frosted so no one could look in from the elevated trains passing by.

On Saturday nights Big Sally opened the basement to selected clients and a gambling casino was running down there. You couldn't get in unless someone vouched for you.

Of course, the local police precinct commanders were taken care of on a weekly basis. They usually were given a few hundred dollars a week, but at Christmas time they each received five thousand dollars to look the other way. And if they requested it for a precinct party a few girls were sent downstairs to "entertain" the police officers, gratis of course. Big Sally ran a very profitable business for Paulie, and the protection she needed was obtained.

Once a week when Rocco went there to collect for Paulie he was treated to someone special. As a single man, he had no qualms going there for both business and pleasure. Even after he was married he didn't stop. He would say it was "a force ah habit".

One of the girls he met there he liked a lot, and offered to set her up in an apartment he would rent for her. She was a young Dominican girl, about nineteen, and was very exotic looking. He had a thing for Latino girls.

She was not very large, but she had a big butt and knew how to please a man. Rocco always asked for her.

One time he was there and after they were finished he sat with her and started to talk to her in a different manner than before.

"Lis'n Alisa, I wan-ta set youse up ina place jus for us," he told her on a visit one day. They had just finished fooling around, and the offer sounded good to her. She figured it was easy money and a free place to crash for a while. Alisa did not plan on it being a long-term affair. Little did she know this arrangement would last for years.

"I'll get us a place and youse can live deer wit me when I have time," Rocco said. This sounded normal to him. He had the extra money for this setup, and he liked her also. She was forbidden fruit, and he could not resist.

Alisa did not mind working in the brothel. If she could land someone like Rocco, even if it did not last, why not work there? She figured "I could always go back to Big Sally when it ended."

Rocco leased a two bedroom apartment for her in Bay Ridge and moved her in after buying all the furniture and stuff she would need at a furniture store called Chrome Furniture Center on Coney Island Avenue, near Big Sally's old place.

When Rocco went into the store to see what they had on display he liked their furniture very much. "Lissen", he said to the owner, "youse got nice stuff here". He bought furniture for every room in the apartment and paid cash for it.

In Rocco's right pants pocket, he kept the fifty and hundred dollar bills. In his left pants pocket, he stashed the twenties and tens. If he was given change and it was fives or less he always gave it back as a tip.

Next week I may be com'in back wit someone else. Youse nev-ah seen me before, right" he told the furniture store owner. He put his hand in his right pocket and took out a fifty-dollar bill. He walked up to the owner and gave it to him. "Here's a tip. Youse did a good job. Tanks". And the subject was never mentioned again.

Alisa thought the setup with him would last until he became tired of her, but eventually, she fell for him, and he with her.

At first, for her, it was the money and security, but over time that relationship changed to love. Eventually, even he developed true feelings for her, and it wasn't just a setup for the sex, but a true common law like marriage. This lasted for decades until his death. She never worked in a brothel again. Alisa did not have to, not because she did not want to. It didn't matter to her. Sex is sex, and if she is paid for it, why not?

Alisa knew better than to ask him to leave his wife. She knew what he did, and was always fearful of knowing too much. She had been with a lot of men like Rocco, always kept her mouth shut, and did not ask any questions. For her own safety, she did not want to know the answers.

Rocco, in his mind, took his marriage vows seriously, and would never even think about divorce. It would be a disgrace to his parents and family if he did. But a girlfriend was something else. That was okay.

Alisa had him when he desired her, and it was often enough that she was never wanting, for anything. She knew a good thing when she had one.

Having a gumar was an accepted practice in this area of Brooklyn.

The two families were kept separate and apart. Gina Marie might have had her suspicions that Rocco was cheating on her, but she knew better than to mention anything.

Gina Marie's four kids were kept well dressed, as was she, and they lived very nicely. New cars, vacations, cruises, jewelry, a large house in Bay Ridge overlooking the Verrazano Bridge, and whatever she felt she needed she is given. Why cause problems?

After Rocco was married to Gina Marie he didn't stop going to the brothels to collect for Paulie. It was still business, sometimes. And Alisa was always available anyway; she was his gumar.

***

Gina Marie took secretarial courses in high school and after graduation applied for a job in Manhattan with a big American bank at their Park

Avenue headquarters. She worked in their back office, on the twenty-first floor as a secretary to one of the bank's vice presidents, Patrick Walsh.

She was with the bank for almost a year when Patrick finally noticed her walking through the hallway going to lunch. He had just broken off with his girlfriend and was looking for someone new. They both entered the elevator at the same time.

Patrick was in his early forties, over six feet tall and very handsome with wavy reddish hair and dressed in his custom-made Brooks Brothers suit. He looked like he was from old money that his family inherited. Park Avenue apartments and Hampton beach estates would have been part of his pedigree, it seemed. But it was all an illusion.

He started to look for her and pay attention as to where she worked on the floor. She was very attractive in her tight clothes, had an outgoing personality, always smiling and worked just down the hall from him.

One day when they met at the elevator waiting for the doors to open he turned to her and invited her to lunch. She was thrilled to be asked out by such a good-looking man and was flattered.

They had a nice time together that day at lunch.

There was a small coffee shop down the block like all Manhattan eateries and specialized in quick service at lunchtime. To her it was a normal place to eat, to him he was slumming.

Coffee shops and luncheonettes are all over Manhattan trying to feed millions of people a day. If you passed by their window in the morning you would see a short order cook flipping burgers on the grill and stacking them sideways at the top of the grill to keep them warm. When lunch time came all he had to do was throw them in the broiler for a few seconds to heat them, and out they flew to the tables. Time is important at lunch because the shops are usually small, and the key to profitability is turnover. Get them in and out as quickly as possible, usually with a full stomach so they will come back tomorrow.

When they sat down at a shiny vinyl covered table with no table cloth he asked her how long she had been working at the bank. If she had any questions about work he told her to "just stop by his office and I would be glad to answer them." He was trying to make a move on her but was going very slowly. This was their first lunch together and he did not want to push things that day. Later, he thought, maybe more.

The next day he asked her out for lunch again.

They were having lunch together at a different place this time and he decided to ask her out to dinner after work, and she accepted. She was only dating Rocco at that time and felt she was free to date anyone she wanted to, especially if her date was an executive at the bank.

When Gina Marie went back to work that afternoon she was very excited. She told her friends at the office about Patrick asking her out. They were all giddy and wished her luck on the date.

"I can't believe he ask't me out," she said. "He is so handsome and refined. I feel kinda funny be'in wit him, but why not" she told the girls in her office.

She had no idea he was only interested in her for one thing, and it was not her intellect. He seemed nice and gentlemanly so she had no idea what his true motives were.

Although she was attractive she did lead a rather sheltered life when it came to boys and dating.

Her only experiences were at church chaperoned dances and teen magazines with the pictures of young leading Hollywood stars on the covers.

That evening Patrick took her out to eat at Carmelo's on West 44th street.

They serve Italian food family style and he ordered whatever she wanted, no matter how much it was. The plates were overflowing with food and she was enjoying every minute of it.

The stuffed mushrooms were delicious, and the chicken parmesan with angel hair pasta was mouthwatering. She enjoyed good food and was having a great time.

Gina Marie was very impressed by him. He wore a business suit and spoke well. And he paid attention to her and seemed truly interested in her life.

Rocco never treated her this way, and she loved every moment of it.

The most Rocco ever spent on her was for a burger and fries, and maybe a movie.

Then they would go for a car ride and park by the bay, near Korvettes Department store, and make out. This was at the foot of Bay Parkway in a huge parking lot overlooking New York Harbor. It was romantic but shared with a dozen other cars parked there too.

But this date, tonight, with Patrick, was different. She knew this was not a cheap date, but a whole lot more expensive. She really liked it, and it seemed like a dream.

Patrick was polished and an executive at the bank. He was a graduate of Wharton in Philadelphia and was being fast-tracked into upper management due to his father's connections.

Gina Marie was just a high school girl from Brooklyn, and this was her first job. She had rarely gone to Manhattan since everything she ever needed was available in Bensonhurst. It was almost like a country farm girl going to the big city for the first time. Patrick was totally out of her league, but she was having a good time and innocently enjoying every minute of it.

After dinner, Patrick asked her if she would like to go dancing. They walked out onto Broadway and hailed a cab. He took her to Rockefeller Center to the Rainbow Room for cocktails.

The live band and the dance floor made for an enchanting evening.

"Would you like to dance?" Patrick asked.

It was a slow number the band was playing, and she agreed. They stood and walked to the edge of the dance floor. He held her tightly against him on the polished parquet dance floor. His right arm pulled her waist close to his and her chest pushed into his, and he was enjoying it, she could tell.

They danced to the center of the floor under the crystal chandelier.

Gina Marie felt a little uncomfortable being so close to him but did not mind. She thought he was so good looking. For a moment she felt like a princess dancing with a prince. But it would not last for long.

She never drank more than a glass of wine in her life, but tonight she ordered a whiskey sour, and he had a top-shelf whiskey on the rocks. Gina Marie heard that a whiskey sour was a sophisticated drink so she drank one.

The room was packed, the tables were small, and there was barely enough room for the waitress to get by everyone sat so close together. Too close as it would turn out.

They had another round of drinks and they started to gently kiss. Patrick bent over towards her, and she leaned in towards him. It was nothing passionate, just a light kiss on the lips.

Gina Marie was not used to drinking strong cocktails, and Patrick was extremely handsome. She was feeling the liquor and was a little light headed by now. Not drunk but friendly and smiling even more than usual. She was giving out signals to him that she really would not send out if she were stone sober.

Slowly he placed his hand on her knee and she gently removed it. It was too soon.

Although she was feeling a buzz from the liquor she was not about to have sex with him right away. She started to really feel uncomfortable.

But he would not be denied. The whiskey was talking and he turned to her and asked, "What is the matter?"

She responded "I jus wen out wit youse tonight for duh firs time. I'm not dat kine-a gurl. It would be nice ta get ta know youse better before any-ting took place" she said.

Patrick was never told no before. There wasn't a girl who ever had said no to him. He was flustered, annoyed, and embarrassed at being told no.

He had been raised in Beach Channel in Queens by Shanty Irish and not the Park Avenue flair he seemed to exude. He had worked hard to get ahead. But he still had that crudeness lying just below that polished educated surface. With a few drinks in him, it came out.

They finished their cocktails in silence, and then Patrick stood to leave without saying a word to her. She followed him out, and they left the club in silence not speaking to one another.

When he walked out of the building he hailed a cab and went home leaving her in front of the building. He never said a word to her. He opened the cab door as it pulled up next to him, and went in. The taxi drove away leaving her at the front of the building not understanding what happened.

She was alone on the sidewalk on Fifth Avenue and needed to walk to the subway by herself.

Gina Marie was pissed by what he did, and she was also a little tipsy from the alcohol.

It was after midnight and she was nervous to be in the city alone at night. She had heard terrible things about late night Manhattan and was terrified to be there without someone being with her. Going to the city during the daytime was one thing, but at night was altogether different.

She started to slowly walk to the subway to go home. If she walked faster she was afraid she would lose her balance and fall.

Walking down the subway steps she held on to the handrail and made it to the platform where her train would arrive. She leaned against the tile wall waiting.

The train ride was uneventful though some young teenage guys walked on the subway car at the DeKalb Avenue station in Brooklyn, and were looking her over. They were wearing torn jeans and had a few gold chains around their necks. Two smiled slyly at her, and she saw mischief in their eyes.

It was very late at night for a nice looking girl to be alone on the subway. The train was almost empty except for the boys, Gina Marie, and two other people. One passenger looked like a homeless person because he was sleeping on the train curled up in a ball and smelled of urine. The other was an older man, dressed in a suit, minding his business reading a newspaper at the other end of the subway car.

The three boys made some remarks to themselves about her and did nothing at that moment.

But her frayed nerves caused her to break out in a sweat just thinking about it. Her makeup started to run and she took out a tissue and dabbed at her forehead. Her eyes averted looking at them but tried to focus out of the corner of her eyes just to be safe.

The boys ignored her and started to walk towards the suited man at the other end of the train. He was a large heavyset man dressed in a suit and standing at the other end of the subway car, and he smelled of money to them. An easy hit and run they thought.

What they didn't know was that he was a former criminal lawyer for the mob who now did real estate closings. He had enough of mob law, and years before left that kind of practice, deciding he would rather sleep nights than worry.

Now he was divorced from his blond decorator wife and working nights.

He became a workaholic, as he had nothing else in his life to do. So it was not unusual for him to be on the subway late at night going home to Brooklyn.

The boys called out to him to give them some money.

In their eyes, they saw an easy mark with some cash and a fancy watch.

Slowly they walked towards him. Teasing him and calling out as they slowly advanced taunts that went unanswered.

The train is rocking side to side as it maneuvered through the tunnel barreling ahead to the next station. They were holding onto the upright posts as they tried to walk forward toward him.

The boys were stalking their prey. Ever so slowly they approached him, enjoying the expected excitement amongst themselves. Their manhood would be exhibited for all to see. They were the hunters and they saw a kill standing there, waiting, as the train went into another tunnel.

They took a few more steps forward and then they suddenly stopped. Not one of them said anything. They just stood in silence for a moment.

The lawyer slowly took his right hand and pulled back his suit jacket a few inches. He never turned his head to look at them. Only his peripheral vision alerted him. He was as confident in himself as the boys were about what they expected to do to him. But things changed very quickly.

They saw the handle of his chrome Smith and Weston pistol jutting out from his belt holster and froze in their tracks. It was a huge gun that he had bought years ago for protection when he left the mob. He carried it every day on the subway with him.

"Jus kidding man, jus kidding" they yelled out to him. "Don't mean nut'tin, man. Jus hav'in some fun, man" they sputtered. They backed away, never taking their eyes off of him. And he just stood there, turning his head, staring at them, waiting. But nothing happened after that.

"Crazy muther fucker," they said to themselves as they backed away.

They walked off the subway car at the next stop.

Luckily, thanks to that unknown lawyer who became their target instead of her, Gina Marie arrived home safely.

***

The next day when she went to work Gina Marie was met by an older gray haired woman from human resources. "I am sorry to tell you this but you don't work in this office anymore," the lady told her in a matter of fact tone. Gina Marie was being she was being transferred to a branch office uptown, in Harlem.

"I'm sorry to tell you this" the woman repeated again, and continued to say in an understanding yet firm voice, "But your position in this building is being terminated, and you have to go to our uptown branch".

"I don't unner stan why I am be'in moved," she asked the human resource lady.

She asked it again in disbelief. "Why," she asked, "am I be'in moved?" and the human resource lady just repeated her answer. But the woman did tell her it came from "upstairs and there was nothing I could do about it."

Gina Marie stood there, thinking, for a moment in silence. Then she realized why she was being transferred. She didn't put out for Patrick, and this was her punishment.

The new office she reports to was in a branch that is almost a two-hour commute for her from her home in Brooklyn.

Gina Marie was very upset about this. She liked working in the headquarters building. Midtown Manhattan was very exciting, and she enjoyed walking around the area and window-shopping during her lunch break.

Bloomingdales was just a few blocks away. She liked to walk through it and shop there when they had sales.

The hubbub of midtown Manhattan was mesmerizing to her. She loved it.

She felt the electricity in the air from all the people rushing about.

Everything was fast and quick.

It would be different in Harlem. There were a lot of black people and her prejudices from the old neighborhood in Brooklyn were coming back to haunt her.

She never had any problems with African Americans. It was her parents and their friends talking crap that came back into her mind to haunt her. And the memory of the New York riots not so far in the past frightened her also.

Gina Marie was upset she had to leave the midtown Manhattan area. And the thought of a two-hour train ride did not go over well either.

The chances of her getting a seat on the subway were near zero, and she knew it. Plus it also meant smelling the odor of urine on the subway cars for two hours each way is too much for her to bare. At night the homeless slept on the trains and some lived in the subway tunnels. They thought nothing of relieving themselves in the subway cars.

She knew she had to do something, but was not sure what she could do if anything. It seemed too far removed from her realm of capabilities.

That night she had dinner with Rocco at a pizza place Rocco knew. She told him about her transfer to Harlem, and why she was being moved. She told him about her innocent dinner with her boss, and how he tried to get her drunk to take sexual advantage of her. Rocco just listened and didn't say anything. He would take care of it for her tomorrow.

The next morning the building lobby was glistening with polished marble floors and walls when Patrick walked entered the building. The doorman in his pressed uniform greeted him when he walked in.

The elevator doors were carved steel and it had a rosewood interior and art deco flair. Everything reeked of high class and expensive decor. This was a restored landmark office building from the roaring twenties. The bank wanted to make an impression on visitors of its strength and stability, and it worked.

While Patrick and a few other people were waiting for an elevator two very large men walked in and stood next to him, yet slightly behind him, perhaps a half step or so.

When the elevator came down, and the doors opened, they slowly walked in with him. Each one of the men was heavyset, stocky, and muscular. Either one of them could almost fill the elevator entrance by his sheer size alone. They were extremely large men. No one else wanted to follow them in, as the two men entered the elevator, and stopped once they walked inside.

The other people waiting sensed that they should not enter. They stood there in the lobby, and all of them decided to wait for the next car. It also helped that the two men just stood by the door when they entered and did not move, blocking the entrance to the elevator car. Nobody was brave enough to ask them to move in so they could enter.

The taller and older one, Jimmy the Basket, wore a baseball hat and his face was scarred very badly. He was wearing a black turtleneck sweater and a dark tan raincoat. He received his nickname due to his height. He could very easily dunk a basketball when he was a younger man. Now he was in his late forties, or so, and more muscular and stocky. Not lean like in his youth.

The shorter younger man, Beanball, was very round, heavy set, and wore a bowler hat two sizes too small. He is given his nickname because he liked to hit people in the head with a baseball bat. It happened twice in his youth when he was in a street gang in the Red Hook section of Brooklyn. Now he was just scary to look at. And very menacing to be with if he was looking for you. If he was holding a bat you didn't want to be anywhere close to him.

They were an odd couple, but they knew how to talk to people in a convincing manner.

They were the only three in that elevator when the doors closed.

As the elevator started to go up Beanball pushed the emergency stop button, and the elevator immediately halted going up.

The elevator music was being piped in. It was so soft, so gentle. It was playing Moon River, elevator music to relax the occupants.

Patrick was going to say something about stopping the elevator when Jimmy the Basket thrust one hand against Patrick's neck and violently slammed him against the back wall of the elevator, choking the air out of him. With his other hand, Jimmy the Basket grabbed Patrick's shirt and held him securely in an upright position. Patrick's feet were swinging slightly off the floor. Jimmy told him to keep quiet or he would break his neck with one short twist.

The soft music was filling the elevator car with carefully selected theme music. The alto sax started to play a lingering soft rift.

Patrick's eyes were now showing terrible fear, and there was nothing he could do to save himself. These two men were absolutely huge and knew what they were doing. They are experienced collectors and enforcers in Brooklyn for Rocco.

Beanball told Patrick "we were very disappointed in your conduct towards a lady friend of ours."

He said Patrick "did not know how to treat a lady."

A new soft melody started to play from the ceiling of the elevator. Piano keys rippled with a gently melancholy tune down into the elevator car.

Beanball took out his switchblade knife, flicked his wrist and Patrick heard the loud click as the five-inch blade flashed open.

Beanball bent slightly down.

He quickly pulled Patrick's suit pants down in one swift motion and then his boxers.

With his left hand, Beanball grabbed and pulled at Patrick's manhood until they were away from his body.

Beanball then placed the flat part of his knife at the base of Patrick's stomach with the blade facing down.

From the speakers in the ceiling came piano music playing another relaxing mood setting tune, yet below it was calculated mayhem.

Slowly Beanball started to move the extremely sharp knife in a downward motion, shaving the hair off Patrick's lower abdomen.

Patrick could feel the cold steel against his lower stomach. The flat part of the blade was now firmly pressed into his lower abdomen's flesh. With just a quick slash the deed would have been done.

Beanball looked up at Jimmy waiting for the go ahead. "Just tell me an I'll go head wit it," Beanball said.

Patrick was now sweating profusely as he nervously sensed what was about to happen.

He tried to squirm, but Jimmy was holding him very tightly. He was at their mercy. His eyes started to roll up toward the ceiling. He clenched his fists apprehensive as to what was about to happen to him next.

Jimmy the Basket slowly put his mouth next to Patrick's left ear and told him "we have a fren who's very upset. Youse made his girl fren leave dis office an got a job in Harlem. We tink dat you should move her back here. Do ya agree, or do we have ta come back an finish our ride wit youse?"

Patrick gurgled something that sounded like a positive answer so Jimmy the Basket removed his hands from his neck and chest. Patrick fell to the floor of the elevator and collapsed, his legs had no strength left in them from nerves.

Stunned with disbelief about what just happened Patrick relieved himself all over his suit pants.

Beanball pulled the stop button back out and pushed the next floor so they could leave. The doors opened and they calmly walked out and went to the stairwell to walk down.

The elevator continued to the next floor, Patrick rushed out and went to the men's room to clean himself.

Twenty minutes later he walked out to the elevator and took it to the lobby. He hailed a cab and went directly home, changed his clothes, and collapsed into a leather easy chair in his living room. After he gathered his thoughts together sitting for an hour, nursing some whiskey over ice Patrick left his apartment, and went back to the bank. He could not stop thinking about what had just happened to him. It was a nightmare come to life. This was the reality of Rocco's world, and Patrick experienced a little taste of it.

By the time the elevator finally reached the twenty-first floor, where his office is, Patrick firmly decided that Gina Marie should not only be moved back to the main building but also given a raise for her troubles.

Patrick Walsh never mentioned the elevator ride to anyone, and to this day Gina Marie has no firm knowledge as to why she has moved around so much that week. But she had an idea that Rocco somehow spoke to Patrick.

Rocco never told her what he did. But Gina Marie knew he did something because Patrick left the building the next day, and she never heard from him again. It was not in her to ask Rocco what he said to Patrick. She never thought to ask, or maybe she knew better than to ask.

She was so happy to be back in midtown that she soon forgot her short stay in Harlem.

Patrick never forgot it, and that afternoon he asked human resources for an immediate transfer to a Queen's branch office near his home. He wanted to get away from Gina Marie as soon, and as far as possible. The closer to Beach Channel the better, he thought.

Gina Marie then started to date Rocco on a continuing and exclusive basis, and finally, after two years, they were engaged.

They were sitting at a ball game at Shea stadium one Sunday afternoon when Rocco turned to Gina Marie. "Maybe we should go fa dinner tonight at Louie's on the bay," he said.

The dinner, a four-course meatball, and spaghetti entre, was good and after they finished Rocco sat back and looked at Gina Marie.

"Gina, youse know I love youse. Will ya marry me?" he asked.

"Of course I will" she answered. "I've been wait-tin a long time for youse ta axe me."

It was not a long engagement before they decided to set a date and get married. Although Rocco loved her he was in no rush to get married. He thought he had time yet, but nature took its course, and things were pushed up.

When Gina Marie announced the engagement it was also a coincidence about the same time she was pregnant. No one is saying which one happened first, but they did get married almost immediately.

But there was to be a big meeting first.

Gina Marie's parents met with Rocco's at Anna Marie's house for a dinner, to discuss things. After a pleasant talk, a date for the wedding was set. They decided not to wait, for obvious reasons, and the following month the marriage took place.

Her parents, Anna Marie and Mario, were not going to have a daughter pregnant, and not be married. They would not be publicly disgraced. They had their honor to uphold.

Rocco knew he had to get married, or else he would be in trouble. And he knew what trouble was.

Although Gina Marie's parents were not directly connected to the mob Mario had friends and relatives who were. Rocco knew this and had no qualms about marrying Gina Marie. He knew better. Besides he loved her and looked forward to having a family like the church said he should.

It was a small church wedding and only the immediate family attended.

Between the parents, siblings and first cousins, almost one hundred people were there.

A dinner was held at a local restaurant and Rocco and Gina Marie set up house in Bensonhurst, near the Bay Ridge border. It was a nice apartment Rocco had found. And it was only a few blocks away from Alisa, for Rocco's convenience.

Rocco settled in as a husband and father and everything seemed fine.

After each baby was born Gina Marie's figure started to grow wider and wider. She especially added inches in her hips and bottom.

She had tried to lose weight and went on many diets. But she was a good cook and every night she made a full dinner for the kids and Rocco if he was home that night and not working. She could not lose any weight so she stopped trying.

Luckily when she was in high school she learned how to sew so she made her own clothes. Gina Marie was not a fashion conscious person, and simple plain things made her happy.

The nuns were right that it was a trade the girls would always have and use. It also was a lot cheaper than to go to the store and buy the extra-large sizes. If she needed a fancy dress for a wedding or something, Rocco always had one custom made for her. He never said no to her about anything she wanted to buy.

After her first child was born she stopped working at the bank and took care of Rocco Junior. That became her full-time job now.

Rocco was making good money with Paulie, and she had no need to work.

They put a safe in the floor under a rug. Rocco was always paid in cash, and the one thing he was taught by the guys was never put anything in the bank that could show up or be traced.

After a few years, he bought two condos in a building nearby, on different floors. And he bought them for cash under Gina Marie's maiden name so they could not be traced back to him.

In the one he did not live in he again put a floor safe in it and hid his cash there under the floorboards and area rug. He also installed a reinforced steel door behind the entry one for security. There were bars on the windows and he had the apartment lightly furnished. There were timers to turn on and off the lights and television so it appeared someone was always living there. Gina Marie knew that he owned a condo in the building, but she was never in it. She assumed, correctly, it was for business.

The other one he had meetings in. He went there to relax away from everybody when he felt the need to get rid of stress, or with one of Big Sally's girls to help with stress relief.

Gina Marie was raised in the church, and she had four kids but stopped having children for health reasons. Otherwise, she would have kept going. She was against abortion, and only stopped when her priest told her it was okay to use birth control due to her health.

Rocco and Gina had four children, three boys, and one girl.

There was also another son but Gina Marie didn't know about him until many, many years later after Rocco had died.

This is how she found out about Rocco's other son.

***

Rocco's wake was set to start at three in the afternoon. About an hour earlier a young man in his thirties came into the Fattachie Family Funeral Home and asked the funeral director if he could have a moment with the deceased. He wanted to pay his respects, as he had to leave, and go to work.

The funeral director said it was okay and escorted him into the room where Rocco was laid out. The coffin was open. The young man knelt down, crossed himself, and said a small prayer.

His face looked like a younger version of Rocco, but taller and very handsome, with a Latino tinged skin color.

His name was Ricardo Junior, and Rocco was his father, Alisa his mother.

It seemed that Rocco had two complete families.

He would alternate holidays with each, his excuse to Gina Marie was business and that he had to travel for Paulie.

His second family with Alisa Santos knew he had another one, but Gina Marie for decades did not know he had a mistress and a secret family.

Rocco was a good father to both families and loved all his children, even Ricardo Junior.

He made sure Ricardo Junior went to college and paid for his education in cash. Rocco was very proud of him. He went on to get two graduate degrees and become a professor at City University in Manhattan. He was not a street person like his parents. They both wanted more for him.

While he was kneeling Gina Marie entered the funeral home to be alone with Rocco before everyone else came in. She was early and did not know anyone else was there.

She saw Ricardo Junior kneeling and did not say anything until he stood up and she looked into his face.

"I am very sorry to hear of your loss," the young Latino man said to her as she stood weeping, dressed in black. He assumed she was Rocco's widow.

"Rocco was a good man, and I will miss him," he told her.

Looking at him Gina Marie wondered how this Latino young man knew her husband, and even more, looked a lot like him. Maybe from work at the construction jobs, he did for Paulie. But when she looked into his face, through her tears, she recognized something about him.

Instantly she knew the secret Rocco had kept from her.

"Youse is his son?" she asked.

"Yes, I am," he said. "I do not mean to upset you."

"My name is Ricardo Junior, and I wanted to say goodbye to my father. I do not want to cause you any more sorrow. You will never hear from me again."

Gina Marie was startled at this news but was not surprised. She knew that Rocco kept odd hours working for Paulie, and she had heard the rumors, people talking about him, and other things.

There were no signs of infidelity, any lipstick stains, or strange phone calls. But there were whispers at family functions, and friends could be overheard talking at the beauty parlor. Now she knew for a fact.

Although she was hurt Gina Marie is a believer in Jesus, forgiveness, the church, and she knew she had to forgive an innocent. That was how she was raised. Ricardo Junior looked more like Rocco than her own sons did.

She was not mad at Rocco, just hurt and bewildered.

She had been going to church for decades and had been talking to the priest privately about her life and her marriage. This is no surprise, but not expected, today of all days.

Gina Marie held out her hand and took his in hers. She could not get over how he looked more like Rocco than her own sons did, she kept thinking to herself. Slowly she brought his hand to her lips and gently kissed the back of his hand. In him, she saw her husband, a young Rocco.

"I loved Rocco my whole life. He wuz every-ting to me" she whispered to him. There is no hatred in her heart, only sadness, and tears flowing from her eyes. She truly loved Rocco. But this did not change things for her. To her, he was a good husband, and she had no complaints about their marriage. She was a simple person that did not see evil, or think that way.

Gina Marie was devastated by Rocco's death, and this news about Ricardo Junior did not help matters. Ricardo Junior was handsome and charming. He spoke kindly to her and understood how upset she was. He sat down beside her, and they had a quiet conversation.

She knew it was not Ricardo's fault that Rocco was a dog. Through her tears and devastation, she saw a kind, gentler, image of Rocco in him. Not the Rocco that did business every day in the grime and dirt of the city.

Her mind went blank, and she sat holding his hand, rubbing it gently. She was holding onto a mirror image of Rocco, and she could not comprehend exactly what happened. She understood, yet did not.

Quietly he stood, excused himself as he had to get to work, kneeled in front of the open casket and crossed himself, said a prayer, and then left.

Only elderly Paulie knew where to find Ricardo Junior and Alisa, but he didn't say anything until months later when Gina Marie asked him about Rocco's illegitimateate son. Paulie told her everything about the relationship. There was no reason not to.

Eventually, she accepted Ricardo Jr. into her life and introduced him to his half-brothers and sisters over a home cooked meal at her house.

When Rocco's estate was settled, and she had time to think about it, she asked Ricardo Jr. if he would like one of his father's rings, to remember him by.

Gina was very good-hearted and took pity on the boy.

She did the right thing.

Chapter 5 -

Years before this happened, when Olga was a young girl about five years old, her family was about to celebrate the Sabbath on a Friday night. They were a young Jewish family living in a two-room apartment behind a small store in Smolensk.

Her father, Julius Levinsky, had just come home from work as a printer and anticipated another quiet and peaceful Sabbath with his family.

As he walked through the front door to his home he stopped to gently kiss his little daughter hello on the top of her head He totally enjoyed the graceful moment of love he had for her within that soft sweet kiss. Then he proceeded to wash before the family sat down for the Sabbath dinner.

Sarah, her mother, had cooked all that afternoon to prepare the food for Friday evening and Saturday. They would eat before he left that night for the synagogue, and after Julius would come home from services Saturday morning.

She was a tall, thin woman. Facially she was strikingly beautiful and had a kind disposition. This evening she is wearing a kerchief with a very small print on it over her hair as is the custom for religious Jewish women and a cotton dress in light blue with small flowers on it. The family is prepared to greet the Sabbath.

When everyone is finished getting ready they sat down at the table together after Sarah lit the Sabbath candles, and said her blessings over them.

"Something smells very good," Julius said to Sarah with a smile as he leaned over and affectionately tapped his little daughter on the cheek.

Quiet reigned as they waited patiently until Joseph opened his prayer book to say the Sabbath blessings before they started dinner. It is a very serene feeling as they prepared to rest from the week's work.

There is a knock on the door, and they looked at each other. Who could it be, they are not expecting anyone tonight.

Sarah thought of the government's secret police. They are everywhere and arresting people for no reason. She knew a few people who were whisked away during the night and were never seen or heard from again. She started to worry. They were all Jews, some even members of the Communist Party. She started to get nervous.

Julius stood and went to open the door, silently expecting the worst.

"Yossi," the Shamus said to Julius in Yiddish as he entered the room, "I am on my way home, and I wanted to ask you to drop off the newspaper to my apartment next week if you could, when you come home from work. I cannot afford to buy it. I need to find some work, maybe there is some advertised in it. I know some of the papers are not printed very clearly, and before you throw it away I would like one."

"Of course I will do it for you. But you know that it is better if the commissar referred you to a job" Julius answered.

"I know, but I work in the schul and everyone knows it. Because I am Jewish and work there I cannot find outside work. Soon they will come, and take me away if I do not work" he answered. "They find any reason to send Jews away".

"I will not forget you. Do not worry about it I will bring you the newspaper" Julius assured him.

Grateful, the Shamus bid "Goot Shabbos" to the family and left.

Julius turned and sat at the table again to continue his prayers. He raised his wine glass, said the blessing on the win, and then the challah.

When he is finished Sarah rose and went to the stove to portion out the Sabbath meal. Quickly she put the food on plates and turned to serve it when it is hot, and it is delicious.

Afterwards, the family completed their after dinner prayers, and they all stood and went to sit on the beautiful handmade sofa that is in their two-room apartment.

Julius's father was a carpenter by trade. He made this custom sofa for them by hand, before he died, when Julius married Sarah. It was his wedding gift to them.

Once they sat together Sarah started to ask how his day went, and what news was there in the newspaper. They could not afford to buy one, but Julius did not have to as he read everything as he set the type. He repeated to her by memory what was in the paper that day.

They made sure their daughter Olga is playing safely in the corner with her only doll and is out of earshot of the conversation. It is very dangerous to talk about how things are in the world around them and have your child tell her friends or teacher in school.

Julius stopped and looked around before he began talking. He turned to Sarah and started to speak to her in a hushed voice when suddenly he heard footsteps outside his front door.

There was a pounding and harsh knocking on their apartment door.

It is the secret police, they briskly pushed the door open themselves, and stormed in. Three solidly built men with pistols drawn stood in the middle of the kitchen.

"Where is Julius Levinsky the printer?" the lead office demanded.

He is a tall, solidly built man, with a very thick neck, and a big mustache. All the officers called him by his rank, Captain, or Captain Bogrov, except one. He knew him since they were young men, and he was the only person who could call him Ivan.

Julius innocently stood up after hearing his name, was immediately grabbed by both of his arms, dragged out of the apartment and into a waiting truck idling outside.

He had no chance to ask any questions, and even if he did there would be no answers.

Julius knew he is in trouble, and hoped they would leave his family alone. They are his main concern now, not what might happen to him.

Back in the apartment two other policemen walk in and join Captain Bogrov.

"What did he do" Sarah shrieked at the captain as the men forced her husband quickly out of his home.

Sarah was distraught as she knew he was not going to come back soon, or if ever. She heard stories of others being taken away to Siberia, or worse, the secret police basement.

"He works for a printer that distributes lies about the state. He will be dealt with" was the answer one of the men, the Starshina, gave to her as he spits on the floor in disrespect.

"But he only works there, he is a printer, he does not write the newspaper," Sarah told him in an anguished voice, with tears welling up in her eyes.

101

"Really" Captain Bogrov harshly said to her. "I think you know too much about what he does."

"No, no. I am just a housewife. I care for my young daughter. Please" she begged.

"I heard enough whining from you," Captain Bogrov said as he quickly raised his right arm over his head, and swiftly with the back of his gloved hand brought it down with full force, and slapped Sarah in the face.

The force of the blow knocked her off her feet, and she tumbled onto the floor hitting her head against the edge of her dining table.

She started to bleed from her nose and mouth where he hit her. Her tooth had sliced into her lip, and she started to bleed. The gash on her head from the table was also bleeding profusely all over the floor. There is blood all over the place now.

"Take her also" he commanded to his men.

Olga is standing silently and watching all of this in the corner. Her little body started to shake from nerves.

"Mamma, Mamma where are they taking you?" she cried out through her tears. Her small voice lost in the world of political psychopaths. The men ignored her pleas.

"My daughter, please, I have to be with her, let me stay" Sarah pleaded in vain as the blood spurted from her mouth and fell onto her dress. "I have to take care of my baby. She has no one else to care for her. Please…" she begged in vain to hearts of ice and deaf ears.

"Don't worry about your daughter, we will take care of her also" was Captain Bogrov's haughty reply. Then he raised his arm and with his gloved hand clenched into a fist he forcefully struck Sarah directly in the face again, breaking her nose and knocking her front teeth onto the floor. She fell to the floor in a limp pile of humanity. Sternly he told her to be quiet, or he will shoot her outside in the street like a dog.

She rose to her knees weeping into her cupped hands. Blood was running through her fingers, down her wrists to her elbow from her nose, and splattering onto the newly washed floor she had cleaned for the Sabbath.

The other policemen grabbed Sarah by her arms and lifted her upright. Then they took her from her apartment twisting her arms behind her back almost breaking them.

Once outside they shoved her, not into the truck with her husband Julius, but the back of a waiting car that is parked behind it.

Olga was crying loudly now, yelling for her mother, but she is ignored. Finally, the Captain could not stand to hear her anymore. He ordered the last police officer in the room to take Olga and bring her out also. He grabbed her by the back of her blouse. He lifted her up and took her outside to the waiting cars. Another officer opened the trunk of the last third police car, threw her in, and slammed the trunk shut.

Then they drove off.

***

When the truck carrying Julius arrived at police headquarters they took him inside and dragged him down a flight of stairs into a dark cinderblock cell in the basement.

There he was tied to a chair, tortured with lit cigarettes on his bare chest and in his ears, had his toes broken with an iron bar, and continually questioned about the newspaper and how the reporters obtained their information. But he could not honestly answer them, as he was only a printer. He just set the type for the newspaper, which was all he did. But that was not what they wanted to hear.

So finally Julius said whatever he thought they needed to hear. He gave them names of people, addresses, whatever they wanted so they would leave him alone.

When they decided, after a few hours they obtained all the information they could out of him, and it was really not a lot of useful information, they left him in the cell for three days still tied to the chair with only one cup of water.

After the third day, they opened the solid steel cell door and literally dragged him out as he was too weak to stand. He was taken to another truck which is parked in the back of the police station and forcefully thrown onto the flatbed in the rear of the truck. It was already filled with about twenty other people. Then they drove to the train station, and everyone was put on a prison train to Siberia.

The boxcar is packed with people who are accused of all sorts of crimes. Some were real, but most were not.

They were all ages and occupations. If someone thought they could gain favor with the authorities they would tell the police a lie, and soon someone else was gone.

The boxcar is filled with soon to be Siberian workers for the government if they survived the train ride.

Julius smelled the perspiration of the people near him, the stench of bodily fluids and defecation, and it turned his stomach. He sat limply on the floor from weakness. The train started to go, and he sat there blankly just staring into nowhere. Quietly, in a faint whisper almost inaudible to even the person next to him, his lips started to move and say the prayer a Jewish person is supposed to say in times of distress and death...Shema...Yisroel....

When the train was out of the town, in the countryside, it stopped to refuel. The guards opened the doors to the boxcar and would ask if anyone needed help. If the response was someone died they would wait until they were a distance from the fuel station and open the doors to the boxcar again. Then they would take out the body and order a few of the stronger prisoners to take it off the train, and carry it a few yards from the train tracks.

They were instructed to leave it for the wild animals to come and devour the corpse.

There is no time to bury anyone, and they did not care either. It would only exhaust the prisoners unnecessarily. Then the train would pull out and start moving again, heading towards Siberia in Eastern Russia.

Julius is never heard from again.

***

Sarah is not taken to police headquarters, but to a small run down looking shack just outside of a residential area of the city, next to a section of deserted forest on an old woodcutter's road. It had been years since anyone had been there, except for the government's secret police

They grabbed her by her arm and pulled her out of the car's trunk. Her legs barely touched the ground as they carried her into the small abandoned house. The Captain opened the door and brought her inside the wooden shack which had been used for ages by hunters in the winter to keep warm, and also the secret police.

It is a very spartanly furnished room with a table and four chairs, and two straw beds in the corners of the room. The cast iron potbelly stove is situated in the middle, and the dirt floor is rock hard with no covering.

The first thing they did is put some wood on the stove to start a fire and lit it to warm the room.

Then they took her to one of the beds and threw her down on it. She did not move.

The Starshina reached down and took the top of her cotton dress in his clenched hands by her front collar, and with all his force he tore it off of her.

She lied there completely naked, her body shivering in the still cold air. The furnace is not yet throwing off heat, but they did not care. She slowly tried to get up, and Captain Bogrov hit her on the side of her left temple causing her to fall back onto the bed dazed.

Although there was a chill in the cabin Captain Bogrov dropped his pants and approached her. The soft whimpering cries coming from her did not distract him. He was focused on only one thing, his sexual satisfaction and the humiliation of this woman. The disgusting cigarette breath from his mouth clouded in the chilled air of the shack as he approached her quivering body.

Sarah is raped by Captain Bogrov first, then his second in command, his boyhood friend the Starshina.

Sexually satisfied they took a baton and sodomised her anally.

When they were finished abusing her with all their perverted fantasies they lifted her up by her hair and dragged her bleeding body outside into the woods. Her heels were dragging on the rocks, and bleeding heavily but they did not care.

Sarah was whimpering from pain in a subdued voice, as her body had no strength left to even scream out at them. They had beaten her into submission with their fists and batons before they acted out their sick sexual fantasies and beat her again when they were finished.

When they had gone a short distance into the dense tree line, they stopped in an area of the forest with heavy underbrush, and let her limp body drop to the cold hard soil of the forest. Then they took out their pistols, and each shot her twice, once in the jaw disfiguring her face, the second in her chest, the third in her abdomen, and the fourth on the side of her head. Then they laughed at what they had done.

They left her lifeless body lying there, and calmly walked away, laughing aloud about what they had just done. She was not human to them, just another Jew.

***

The third car with little Olga was driven to a local orphanage, and she was dropped off there as a ward of the state, but that was not the original order.

The officer driving the car was instructed to drive to a local bridge, and throw her into the strong currents of the icy river below to drown. But no one knew he had a little daughter also. He could not bring himself to do the killing of a child. So he made a slight detour and went to an orphanage he knew would take her in. Especially if a police officer brought her there, no questions would be asked.

The woman in charge surmised what had happened to Olga's parents as many of the other children who were brought there through the years by the secret police also were the result of "permanent arrests".

She knew better than to ask any questions, only what is the child's name, and age. That is all she needed for her records. The more children she took in the more the state paid her to care for them. And the more she could skim off the money for herself, and keep hidden.

Olga is raised in that orphanage along with give or take forty other children. It is located just outside of Smolensk.

Although it was drab and dreary looking and had a solidly communist institutional look, it basically did what it is supposed to do. It raised good Soviet Citizens loyal to the state without any parental influence. That is why it is allowed to remain in use.

It was fairly remote, yet it is not too far from the train station.

When the freight trains rumble past the orphanage the floorboards would rattle from the weight of the steel wheels grinding heavily on the iron tracks. As she grew older Olga would hear the locomotive huffing at night as it passed by the area, and she would dream of leaving on it one day.

In school, she had always been very athletic, and participated successfully in track and field, and tried out in some gymnastic classes, but she was too tall for that to last. The politburo had wanted to train girls to compete in the Olympics, and they tried out all teen girls, including Olga. She excelled in track and field and was a long distance runner. Her stamina and mindset drove her to excel.

As a teenager, she had a crush on a boy named Pyotr who lived nearby with his family and they went to the same school. He would sit with her at lunch, talk to her and a friendship quickly developed.

Soon it became more than a friendship and a bond was developing between them. When they had a chance they would walk in the woods and become very close, physically. As teenagers, their hormones were raging and were not to be denied.

For the first time in her adult life, that she could remember, she felt wanted, and she enjoyed the feeling. The days dragged on and she could not wait for school to end so she could be with Pyotr again.

He started to bring her things, rings, necklaces, and sometimes a nice scarf. Olga did not ask where they came from. It never crossed her mind to ask. His father was a local commissar and a high communist official. Somehow he is given advantages, and bribes, that others did not get. And Pyotr took advantage of that fact. But he never realized he was being followed.

One afternoon when they were planning to be together a police officer came to the school and waited nearby for them to walk into the woods. The policeman was a tall stocky man with a large mustache, and had been on the police force for many years. Captain Bogrov knew how things worked and was the recipient of many illegal offers himself. He was caught stealing from the police monies, and Pyotr's father had demoted him back to a private, instead of sending him to Siberia.

He was resentful and vowed to get even with the commissar. He followed Pyotr as he and Olga slowly walked into the heavily wooded forest, and tried to lose themselves amongst the trees. When they stopped walking, he approached them.

"Pyotr" he called out to him. "I have been watching you, and I know you have a lot of money, and where you get it also. I know who your father is, and I want some now" he demanded. He walked over to

Pyotr and stared at his face, not smiling, just staring into his eyes.

Pyotr just stood there, frozen. He realized he was in big trouble, and could be sent to a work camp, or worse, a Russian prison. This officer will lie, and get him and his father in trouble.

"What do you want to do with me?" Pyotr asked the officer.

"I am not a greedy man" is his response. "Pay me half of what you have, or I will have you and your girlfriend arrested. Then I will have sex with her in the police station, and share her with the other officers" he told Pyotr.

Pyotr knew that corruption was rampant in Smolensk. He started to walk towards the police officer to see if he would take some jewelry Pyotr had on him, as a bribe, when the officer silently drew his gun and shot him at point-blank range. The shots rang out through the forest. Stunned, Pyotr looked at him in disbelief and then collapsed onto the ground, choking on his own blood, slowly dying.

"I will take all your things, and her too," he said to him as Pyotr fell mortally wounded. "I changed my mind," Bogrov said with contempt in his voice.

He now turned his attention to Olga and grabbed her by her hair and flung her to the ground. Slowly he approached her. He intended to rape her right there while Pyotr lay wounded, bleeding to death, watching helplessly.

As he came closer, looking into his face, Olga had a flashback to the night her family was destroyed by this man. Suddenly she recognized him. The memory is hazy but she knew he was evil.

But the noise of the shots had attracted other students from the school, and they started to run into the forest yelling, trying to see what had happened.

Bogrov told her to get up, and not say a word of what happened, or he would shoot her also.

"Tonight I will meet you at the orphanage at eight. Then I will deal with you. Be there" he said with a firm order, "or else".

So he let her get up, and she quickly left the area while he deftly went through Pyotr's pockets, as he lied motionless on the ground, gasping for breath.

That afternoon at the police station Bogrov reported that three men in the forest had attacked Pyotr, and when he came to help there was a shooting and Pyotr was shot by one of the men.

There are no ballistic tests in this part of Russia, so the officer's word is taken as the truth. Plus he shared some of Pyotr's jewelry with his Colonel.

That night Olga walked out of the orphanage, and met him at exactly eight, in front of the building. She felt that she had to go with him or she would be next to be shot.

Olga knew what he wanted from her, and she had a plan to protect herself.

If she did not do as he asked she would be taken to the police station and never heard from again. This is how things happened in Russia. She believes he told no one what he is going to do this evening with her.

He is waiting in an unmarked police car parked a few yards away from the entrance to the orphanage.

Slowly she walks over and enters in the back seat as she is instructed to do. Then he drove off to a dark deserted area near the forest, at the edge of town. There he stopped by the abandoned woodcutter's shack, where those years before he had raped and killed her mother. But the roof had caved in and he could not enter it. He would have to use the car for tonight.

There are no streetlights here only the light from the moon and the stars above. There is not a cloud in the sky, and the silence of the forest is deafening.

When he finally stopped driving and parked next to the shack, he walked out of the front seat and around the back of the car, opened the rear door, and told her to undress.

She did as he asked while he stood outside watching her.

Olga was sitting up against the opposite back door waiting for him to enter the car. When he dropped his slacks and prepared to get in the back of the car, he saw she was already undressed and waiting for him.

He looked at her naked, and her long hair in the moonlight shining through the rear window. Her motionless body sat there waiting for him. But he did not see, in the darkness, the butcher's knife she had taken from the kitchen at the orphanage. She dropped it down below the seat when she sat in the car. Now she was holding it in the darkness, the knife almost touching the floor, pressed against the side of the seat bottom, waiting for her revenge, both for Pyotr whom she cared for, and unknowingly, for Sarah her mother.

Slowly he crept in the back seat toward her outstretched legs.

He carefully approached her, as the seat was not wide enough for him to fully crawl on, and he bent over her with his tongue sticking out and his body odor reeking in the night air. Then he saw her exposed chest glistening in the moonlight, and his body was filled with anticipation.

Olga could smell his disgusting cigarette breadth, as her mother did years before. He was now older, breathing heavily as he climbed into the car, and came close to her.

His nude unwashed body gave off an odor that repulsed her. She sat still, waiting, looking at him, emotionless, and waiting for the time to strike. He crawled ever so slowly, closer and closer to her chest. She felt time had almost stopped, and she mentally saw him come towards her in slow motion.

Bogrov was now so close he was about to put his lips on her chest, in anticipation of abusing her sexually. But he was not her Pyotr, and he would pay dearly for his actions.

At this precise moment, Olga quickly raised the knife from below the seat and swiftly slashed at his neck. Once, twice, three times until he stopped moving forward and realized what was happening. He started to spit out blood and was having trouble breathing.

He tried to back out of the car but Olga grabbed him at the top of his thick hair and held his neck up while she slashed again and again in a rage of fury.

The Police Officer Bogrov had killed her lover, and now he was going to pay for it.

Desperately trying to back out of the car he was stopped by Olga. She spread apart her muscular legs against each of the car's rear door pillars for stability. As he tried to pull away she was straining, trying to keep him in the car, as she continued to slash at his throat and face. The knife tore through his cheeks, his lips, and his throat with unleashed fury.

His blood was now spurting out over her body and also completely covering the back seat. It is seeping under her sweaty straining body causing her muscular back to slip on the seat when finally with one last gasp of life he managed to break her grip and went out the rear door falling to the ground. She is left holding a tuft of his hair in her hand.

He was lying on the ground, on his back, almost motionless as his chest was heaving for breath with his arms outstretched and his chest soaked in blood. His lungs had filled with blood, and he is drowning in his own bodily fluid.

But it was too late for him to escape. The knife strikes found their mark and were fatal.

He slouched over into a fetal position and rolled downwards, lifeless into a dirt ditch, near the edge of the tree line.

Olga quickly went out the other car door, ran to the other side of the car, and looked at his still body. Standing over him she felt nothing for him. There was no humanity in him that she could see.

She pulled on her pants and tried to get dressed.

Olga ignored the blood that had bathed her body in his fight for life. She had no time, or place, to clean off.

She buttoned up her blouse and started to run back to the orphanage using the moonlight to see the road. Fortunately for her, she is a runner and used her stamina to get back before dawn.

When she was halfway back she threw the knife away, deep into the forest, where no one would ever find it.

She entered the back door to the orphanage, by the basement. Olga changed her clothes using someone's clean clothing that is in the laundry room and hid her bloody clothes inside a laundry bag full of unwashed clothes. She took the bag with her to her room to wait till later when she will wash them, and nobody would find out.

The blood had dried on her by now and it did not stain the borrowed clothes. Quietly she walked upstairs to have her morning shower before others awoke, and join everyone in time for breakfast.

This was her first kill, and she felt nothing except revenge. No remorse, no bad feelings, nothing.

A month later when the police eventually found what was left of the body of Bogrov they had no idea who killed him. The animals of the forest had devoured him as they did Sarah years before. He did not report to anyone he is going anywhere that night, and there are no leads. It is another unsolved crime which was buried in massive paperwork.

Pyotr's body had been found against the tree where Bogrov said he had heard gunshots. They thought he had entered into a gunfight with criminals, and again, there were no leads so they forgot about it. That is not unusual.

Pyotr's father had a large funeral for him, and his son was awarded a medal for bravery for fighting off criminals.

***

Soon after the funeral Olga finished high school and enlisted in the Russian Army in order to leave the area. There is nothing to keep her here except bad memories.

The enlistment officer gave her a train ticket, and she is off to basic training in the Russian army.

Basic is not too hard for her as she is in very good condition from running track in high school. She kept up with the men running in basic training, and was an excellent marksman. That is where she is noticed and brought to the attention of the KGB.

The KGB needed young women who could act as spies and assassins. There are enough men in their ranks, but they are lacking in young women who are attractive and willing to do this type of work.

A KGB recruiter is visiting the army base when he heard of Olga from the sergeants in the mess hall. They were amazed that she is also excelling in hand-to-hand combat and had the stamina of a man.

The recruiter went to speak to her and asked if she would like to serve her country with honor, but in a very dangerous field. She said she would agree to do anything for Russia, and is ready whenever they wanted her.

The same afternoon she is discharged from the army and driven overnight by the recruiter to Moscow.

It is then, in KGB headquarters in the Kremlin Viktor first met her, and personally saw to it that she was properly trained.

One of the things she is taught and excelled in, is how to kill in hand-to-hand combat in close quarters. Plus she is instructed in other forms of lethal close encounter combat and explosives. For over one year she is intensively trained and taught how to survive in very difficult conditions.

Viktor also took more than a casual business interest in her.

Olga is tall, good-looking, and had an excellent command of English which she learned in high school. Her hair is now long and falls down her back just below her shoulders. She usually wore it in a ponytail when she is in training.

It did not take very long before they would soon become lovers.

The fact that he is much older than her did not seem to matter to either of them. She felt wanted for the first time since Pyotr, and also protected by Viktor. The feeling of being emotionally secure would probably be a better description of her relationship with Viktor.

Her first foreign assignment was to London.

Viktor had sent for her to meet him at his office one afternoon.

The office is surprisingly plush for a communist official. When he took over the branch of the secret police he ordered what he wanted without any regard to cost. As the head of the unit that trained and sent out assassins nobody wanted to get on his wrong side.

"Good morning Olga" he greeted her as she walked into his private office, and kissed her.

"I have a new mission for you in London. This will be your first foreign trip as a diplomat. My secretary will give you your papers when you leave, with your travel plans included" he said.

"Once you arrive in London I want you to stay at The Berkeley Hotel at Wilton Place Knightsbridge. It is near the British Library and Kensington Palace. Your assignment will be sent to you once you arrive and check in. A messenger from the embassy will meet you at the hotel, and then you will go to the British Library the next morning. Make sure you bring your tools with you. They will not be searched as your luggage will have diplomatic seals on them" he continued.

Although this was her first mission outside of Russia, it was not her first assassination, and she was very calm and matter of fact about it.

She flew into Heathrow Airport the next day and checked into a very nice room. It is a typical staid British style room in a better hotel. She unpacked and took a quick nap before she went out for a bite to eat.

There was a gentle tap on her door the next morning, and she arose to open it.

"My name is Matvei and I have a letter for you," he said in Russian.

He knew it was Olga as a picture was sent to him along with the letter so it would go to the right person.

"Thank you" as she took the letter, and closed the door.

Her instructions were to convince a defector that it would be better to come back to his country, or his wife and two daughters would be killed. If he refused, then she was to terminate him.

It said that he has been followed, is writing a tell-all book in the British Library, and will be selling it to the highest bidder. It would be either the British or American spy agencies, or the newspapers. He expects them to give him a lot of money, and a new identity. But they do not know that he defected yet. Only Viktor does as he sent him on a mission, and he disappeared. The Russian embassy staff spotted him, and now it is Olga's job to finish him off.

After reading it Olga took it into the bathroom and burned it before dropping it in the toilet, and flushing.

She changed and went downstairs to have something to eat. It is already midafternoon, and she is hungry.

Olga walked to Clarks at 124 Kensington Church Street for some food and a beer.

Then she waited till late afternoon reading in her hotel room. Just before five o'clock she packed her "tools" and passport and walked to the library to look for her target.

She is to go the next morning, but she thought she would look the place over before she went in, and took care of things.

As she entered the main lobby she saw some beautiful mahogany reading rooms facing St. James Square. She meandered in to look around, and suddenly, in the corner sitting at a table writing. Olga saw her target.

She walked into the reading room, and sat two tables away, facing him.

There were only a few people in the room at that time, as many of them packed up and went home for dinner about thirty minutes before.

She did not want to approach him in there as they installed video cameras everywhere, so she waited until he stood later to leave.

He finished writing, and packed his notes into a travel bag, stood up, and walked out onto the bustling street.

Olga followed him as best she could, as there were hundreds of people walking about. When he stopped at the corner she walked up behind him, and in Russian told him not to move or she would kill him right there on the street.

"Walk across the street, and stop next to that building, in the doorway. I want to talk to you," she told him and followed from behind.

He knew who had sent her, and why.

Once they crossed the street she asked him "don't you care about your wife and daughters? You left them behind in Russia."

"Who cares about them" was his disdainful answer. "That fat General Lagunov forced me into marrying his daughter. I was in the army as a private, and I stole some surplus food to sell on the black market. I was caught, and going to Siberia for five years. He was in the court when my trial was going on, and he told me he could pardon me if I married his daughter. I thought how bad could it be?"

"When I saw her for the first time it was too late to back out. She had more hair on her face than

Castro has in his beard. I am not going back. I don't care what you do to them" he with finality.

"You know," Olga said, "I have to report back to the Kremlin. I do not know what they will do to them once they hear about what you told me". She tried once more to convince him.

"That is her problem, and her fathers, too" was his response to her.

As Olga took out a cigarette from her pocket she asked him "Listen, I need a light, do you have one?"

He opened his overcoat and reached in to get his lighter. When his heavy coat was opened Olga acted as if she tripped, and fell onto him. The knife in her hand swiftly cut through his shirt, between the ribs, and into his heart. She twisted it hard to the left, and then to the right, pushing him back against the wall, and took the knife out quickly. His thick overcoat shielded the massive bleeding from passing pedestrians possibly seeing it. He leaned back, a blank look on his face, as he slowly slid downwards toward the ground.

Olga turned around and calmly walked away holding his notes as he took his last breath of life.

She stopped a cab and rode silently to the airport where she boarded a plane for Warsaw Poland. There she would stay at the Russian embassy until arrangements were made to fly her back to Moscow.

***

She was sent on many internal missions for the KGB, and always completed them successfully.

When Viktor eventually "retired" from the KGB and immigrated (transferred?) to the United States, Olga came with him.

This is how she ended up living in Brighton Beach Brooklyn with Viktor.

The money that Viktor used to build his criminal organization in Brighton is a mystery to many people. There are only two or three people in the Kremlin who actually know how he came to America with funding.

Chapter 6 –

She was a tall, curvaceous, olive-colored skinned girl like her grandmother. She wore her light brown hair short and was a loud, big mouth, Italian girl from Brooklyn. She also had the fiery temperament and the astounding good looks of her late grandmother Theresa Avila.

Mary Catherine was a middle child and owned all the typical traits that one would expect from a middle child. She was a loner, did not form many close relationships with friends, and was also very creative. Sometimes she was even rebellious, like the time in high school she dated a Jewish boy.

Sam did not look Jewish. He was blond, had bright blue eyes with long shoulder length hair and was very cute looking. He went to Lincoln High School on Ocean Parkway. She really fell for him when she saw him walking on 13th Avenue. They went to the movies a few times and out to eat afterward, but nothing really happened. Just some kissing and light petting when they sat in the back of the balcony at the movies. Mary Catherine really liked Sam and at night she would dream about them getting married, and living in a big house in Bay Ridge. But dreams are not reality.

When she finally told her mother about Sam she was admonished "good Catholic girls do not date Jewish boys. That is not why you are going to parochial school." So it was the end of seeing a Jewish boy for a while. But she never forgot him.

When she went to high school she often imitated her older sister Gina Marie. Her plaid uniform skirt was rolled up at the top so the bottom edge was above her knees, and she hung out on the corner where her sister did when she was younger. This is where the boys are located.

And when Mary Catherine was in class she often asked to go to the bathroom. But would sneak out the side door of the school, smoke a cigarette, and talk to the other girls cutting class. She put some index cards by the door lock so it would open when she wanted to get back in. After she was finished smoking she would lift up her shirt and put the cigarette pack back in her underpants so it didn't show. Luckily she sat in the back of the class due to her height, and the elderly nuns never smelled the tobacco scent on her clothes.

Mary Catherine was also very impulsive and often was truant from school, and slightly disrespectful to the nuns. When she played hooky from school she would meet her new boyfriend Carlo, and they would go to his parent's house.

Both of his parents worked so the house was empty during the day. Carlo would "borrow" an adult video from his older brother's room, and they would try to imitate what was being done in the movie. It was a miracle she did not get pregnant considering they had no idea about using condoms. It was never taught in school, and in the pornographic movies, they did not use them.

Carlo was a nephew of a major "Godfather" and everyone knew it. All during Mary Catherine's last two years of high school they had this lustful encounter every Wednesday afternoon after school, or when they both cut out from school for a whole day.

It was not unusual for Mary Catherine's parents, Anna Marie and Mario, to be summoned to school in the evening, and meet with the Mother Superior about her manners and truancy.

Not that she was extremely rude or cursed at the nuns, but she basically ignored what they said, and did her own thing. This drove the sisters crazy, and they were not going to put up with it. They dared not strike her as she was tall, and had a wild look in her eyes when she was excited, like her grandmother Theresa Avila. The nuns had all decided that they were going to try to be the boss, not Mary Catherine.

This struggle of wills went on for four years until she graduated and left school. It was a tossup who celebrated more when she left, the nuns or her when she received her diploma.

But for four years her parents were endlessly coming to school to meet the principal and the sisters.

Unbelievably Mary Catherine was never expelled. Her grades were okay, the school needed the tuition, she never disrupted a class, and enrollment was down. Which one was the deciding factor that kept her in school is up for debate. But she stayed in the school until graduation.

After Mary Catherine graduated from high school she didn't want to work in an office like her older sister so she applied for a job selling at a local general store in the neighborhood.

In the mornings she would stock the shelves and in the afternoon she would help the customers when they came into shop. She worked there for many years.

It was just right for her.

She was able to meet a lot of new people, and she often joked around with the customers. As an outgoing young girl, she sold more items than the older white-haired reserved Italian ladies that worked there. The other women were somewhat miffed that she sold more, but they somehow seemed to all get along. Nothing was ever said to her personally. They just talked about her behind her back.

Most of the women that worked there were widows and always dressed in black. Mary Catherine is the youngest and one of the few who was not married dressed in the styles of the day. Bright colors and go-go skirts hiked up really high. Her co-workers used to talk about how high her skirts were, and that when she bent over to pick something up, you could see her business. Gossip was the rule, not the exception in that small store.

***

One day one of her older co-workers came in and said that "Bernardo the shoemaker", who had a small repair shop two doors down, "is keeping a young girl in the back of his store." This is scandalous to this particular woman. She never heard of such a thing in her life, and could not wait to tell the other ladies she worked with.

She had stopped in to have a pair of shoes resoled, and she saw this young girl walking around in the back of his shop. The woman knew Bernardo was married, and this girl looked Spanish to her, not Italian.

Bernardo was in his late forties, a hairy man with large muscular arms that served him well when he was working with thick leather soles. The lathe in his shop was over forty years old and is a belt driven model that made clickity sounds as it turned the different grinding wheels. The pot of glue that was attached overflowed with dried glue that had dripped down the sides. Hand cutting and forming the thick leather soles, and then grinding them till they were smooth took effort. His forearms were thick and strong.

He was not particularly attractive, and in his youth did not date a lot. He was married (it was arranged by their parents) and he had two young daughters.

His wife was a large heavyset woman, unkempt, and neither of them dressed fashionably or even had a sense of style. They were working class and looked it. They both were from solid peasant stock back in the old country and also spoke Italian, besides their broken English.

One day this very young Puerto Rican girl, who was walking the streets and homeless, wandered into his shop looking for a handout. She looked eighteen but in reality was only fourteen years old. She was dressed in tight jeans and her blouse was unbuttoned halfway down. Her black hair was down past her shoulders, was full and wavy, and her mildly colored Latino skin color was set off by as it framed her face.

She was looking for money for food, and she went door to door asking for donations. The girl was willing to do anything for money. Then she came to the shoe shop and met Bernardo.

"Hi," she said as she opened the door to his shop, and walked in. "I need some change for food, and wondered if you can help me out?"

"Sure I can help" Bernardo answered. "Maybe we can help each other out," he said.

He offered to buy her food, a place to stay overnight (in the back of his shop), and in return, she would service him sexually. She was hungry and it did not take long to agree to his terms. Besides, it was getting late, and she needed a warm place to stay for the night.

She had been on the streets for almost six months and this arrangement is like ones she had had before.

It was a teacher named Phil from a high school near Atlantic Avenue in downtown Brooklyn who took her in for a while. The high school used to be an all-girls school. It was not unusual for some of the male teachers, of all ages, to have an affair with the young Spanish girls who were students there. Plus in the Latin American culture where they came from young girls often went with much older men. It was security for them in a society that was poor and did not have many social services.

The students were from a lower social demographic area and were easy to score with. With over a few thousand girls there you could count the virgins on one hand.

Phil would take her into his classroom during lunch for "private tutoring," lock the door and have sex with her in the rear of the room. She liked the attention he was giving her, and she always passed every test he gave in class. Plus Phil would give her money every day as sort of an allowance so she would keep coming back to him for sex. She bought records on Fulton Street after school with the money he gave her. Sometimes when he gave her more she went to clothes shopping at Mays or Klein's on the Square.

But he was not the only teacher she had sex with. And a lot of the younger male teachers also had their pleasurable moments with her. That is how she was passing all her classes, dressing very nicely, and rarely attended a class. She excelled at sex and often was with more than two or three teachers any given day.

One day Phil decided to sneak her into his parent's house early one afternoon after school and keep her all to himself instead of sharing her with the other teachers. He enjoyed her sexually way too much for his own good.

He kept her in their finished basement where his parents would not see her. They rarely went downstairs as they no longer entertained much, and had no need to go down there anymore.

He brought her food and blankets at night, then slept with her till he woke up in the morning, and went to work.

During the day, she stayed home from school. When his parents were out working she would shower, watch television, and eat whatever was in the frig or cabinets for breakfast and lunch.

When he arrived home from school about two in the afternoon they would have sex again in his bedroom before his mom came home.

He was getting married soon to a nice Jewish girl he met at Brooklyn College. A few days before the wedding he knew she had to leave. He had a problem and was not sure how to handle it.

He wanted to continue the relationship but did not know where she could stay hidden any longer. So he went to his bank one morning, withdrew some cash, and gave her a hundred dollars in small bills. Then he took her to Kings Highway, near his parents' home, where there were plenty of women's clothing stores. He bought her new jeans, two blouses, and a jacket to wear.

They walked to the subway station near Dubrow's Cafeteria where he kissed her goodbye under the subway trestle, at the bus stop, before he turned and went through the token stalls to get on a train.

Then she was on her own.

She walked along Kings Highway for a while, window-shopping, and not really thinking about anything in particular except where to go now. She decided to go back to her stepfather's apartment where she had left some clothes. But it was not a great idea and did not last long.

She left home once before after her mother, Dominica, died from a drug overdose. Dominica had been on drugs since she was twelve and became pregnant at thirteen. She was not sure who the father of her daughter was since she prostituted herself to supply her drug addiction. When she was seventeen she married a John she had met who said he would take her in, and feed her habit.

It was not a marriage that was officiated at but a common law type of arrangement. She just moved in with him and they said they were married.

Dominica really did not know much about her new common-law husband except he kept her doped up and fed her and her daughter. He worked nights with some drug gang in Brooklyn. Eventually, she died from an overdose of bad heroin when her daughter was a young teenage girl.

Dominica's teenage daughter continued to live with her stepfather until he had beaten her once too often in a drunken rage and then raped her. With nowhere to turn and too young to be knowledgeable of what help the city had to offer her, she lived on the streets as best she could.

She was a survivor.

***

This arrangement with Bernardo lasted for almost a week. He would bring her breakfast when he opened his shop, and then later when it was almost lunchtime he would lock the front door. He put an "out to lunch" sign on the glass door, and went to the rear of his shop, behind a short wall, to be with her privately. Then they would have sex. When he was finished he would go out and buy them both freshly made deli sandwiches and bring it back to eat together.

But she had to go when Bernardo's wife, one morning, said she was bringing in some shoes later that day for her girlfriend for him to repair.

Not wanting to lose a good thing he called Rocco. They had grown up together, and as young teenagers, they hung with the same crowd, although they were not close friends.

Bernardo suggested he come into the shop and speak to this girl about working in the brothel above the candy store. That was how he thought he could have his cake, and literally eat it too. To Bernardo, this was a real baccala, and he wanted more. If he could set her up in the brothel he could see her often. But he needed Rocco to make the arrangements.

That afternoon Rocco came to Bernardo's shop see her.

"Rocco" Bernardo said acknowledging him when he came into his shop, "here is the girl I spoke to you about." She slowly walked to the front of the store when she heard Rocco's name.

"What's yer name," Rocco asked.

"My friends call me Star" she replied. She looked at him and knew what he wanted, and she was willing to give it. Star knew that all men wanted the same thing. It did not take her too long in her short life to figure this out.

Bernardo told her Rocco is a very important man and could set her up where she could make a lot of money.

"Lutz go to duh back of duh shop for a while," Rocco told her expecting to be serviced. And he was.

"Lis'sen Bernardo," Rocco said when they were finished. "I'm tak'in her ta meet Big Sally, down da block. I'll talk ta youse later" he said as they walked out the door.

Then he took her by the arm, and they walked down 86th Street a block or two and went to meet Big Sally above Bucky's candy store.

They walked into the candy store and went to the back, then upstairs through the heavy iron door. Rocco had the passkey and was able to enter whenever he wanted to.

Big Sally was introduced to her and she explained the rules of the house, and how things worked there. How much she would be charged for room rental, food, and what Big Sally expected her to make each day. The young girl understood and agreed to stay. She really had no choice unless she wanted to sleep on the street.

She was given a room, condoms if she cared to use them, and would be able to live there if she wanted as she had nowhere else to go.

With the money she earned, after Big Sally deducted for her expenses, she was able to eat and buy clothes. She was doing pretty well for herself there.

Big Sally took extra good care of her as she is very young, and expected that she could become a real money maker for her as she became older. She took a liking to the kid in many ways. Some ways were very motherly, some were as a lover.

Star and Big Sally started a sexual relationship which was beneficial to both of them.

Over time Star settled in, and was very comfortable working there. She became a top money earner and Big Sally's most frequent lover. Her only competition in Big Sally's bed was from Big Sally's boyfriend. After a threesome one afternoon, she was asked to join them frequently in bed, and the competition just faded away.

Rocco and the Madam had their shoes repaired and polished by Bernardo for free for many years after that. And Bernardo was able to continue to see Star at Big Sally's whenever he had the time or urge.

***

In Bensonhurst, the barter system thrived because it was tax-free.

So after hearing the gossip about Bernardo, Mary Catherine just had to go have her shoes repaired, and polished. "I'll be back in a second" she called out to her manager. With that, she scooted out the door and walked briskly to Bernardo's to look in and see what the girl looked like.

When she entered the store she didn't see the girl but heard some rustling in the back behind a thin wall that came out into the shop about seven feet.

Then this beautiful young Puerto Rican girl with flowing long hair walked out to go to the toilet, and Mary Catherine quickly glanced at her but did not get a very good look. She thought she was extremely pretty and young, but couldn't understand why she would stay with Bernardo.

This was enough to somewhat satisfy her curiosity. She left and went back to the store to work, and continue with the gossip about Bernardo with her co-workers.

***

Often on her walk home after work, she would usually stop in the butcher shop, and buy fresh cold cuts, chicken or steak for her mother to cook for dinner. She also liked to have fresh bread or rolls so she would stop in the bakery too. And of course, the fresh cut imported Italian cheeses were delicious.

Finally, the day came, and her boyfriend, Carlo, asked her to marry him. But first, he had to ask her parent's as was the custom.

Mary Catherine told her parents Carlo is coming over to talk to them, and he asked her to marry him. She accepted, but told him she could marry, but only if her parents approved. She knew they would, so she set up this evening meeting for them to get together so he could formally ask them if he could marry her.

That evening Carlo came to the house and went upstairs to meet Anna Marie and Mario. They all sat in the living room on the vinyl covered red velvet sofa and loveseat with the white painted wood trim and started to talk. The air-conditioning was not on, and Carlo was nervous and sweating. His shirt started to stick to the back of the vinyl on the sofa, and he felt uncomfortable.

The light bounced off the crystal droplets that hung from the baroque brass table lamps and was catching Carlo's eye making him squint often.

Mary Catherine thought he was just winking at her during the meeting.

Anna and Mario knew him for many years as he had dated their daughter since high school, and they liked him very much.

When he asked for Mary Catherine's hand in marriage Anna Marie stood from the plastic covered sofa and hugged him. She welcomed him into the family, and couldn't wait to call her friends to tell them the good news.

Carlo was a Don's nephew, and she knew that meant her daughter would be taken care of financially.

Anna Marie was never told by her mother, Theresa Avila, what had happened to her in Sicily by a Don's son. To Theresa's dying day no one knew that she had been raped or what she had done to defend her honor.

She was afraid that if the news of what she had done was known it eventually would reach back to Sicily. Then she and her family would be killed. The mafia has long arms.

A wedding had to be planned, and Anna Marie went to her church the next morning to meet with the priest about holding the wedding in the church. She was told that since she and Mario were members of that parish there would be no problem. But first, he had to meet with Carlo and Mary Catherine, and talk to both of them about raising a family in the church.

He wanted to make sure they would want to have children, and they will be sent to parochial school like all of Anna Marie's girls did.

He brazenly asked Carlo "Are you impotent because the marriage has to produce children." The old priest did not beat around the bush and wanted a direct answer. Carlo sat back in his chair and said to his knowledge he is not.

"Also the both of you have to take a marriage preparation course the church offers" the priest continued. Both of them agreed to go and asked how much money the course is going to cost. The priest answered their question and told them the date the next marriage prep class is being held. Having gone to parochial school there is not much they felt they had to be prepared for, but they did not want to upset the priest so they agreed to everything he asked.

Of course, they both lied to the priest and said they never slept or lived together. If they told the truth it would only delay things a while, and caused them to pay for some other expenses they did not need.

Carlo is not a big person. He is rather thin, brushed his hair straight back, and is about average height. He has the look of a weasel and the same morals. But he is very much in love with her, and especially liked the sex.

Unlike her sister Gina Marie who did not have Rocco use condoms, Mary Catherine took birth control pills and hid them in her closet from her mother. She wasn't about to get pregnant like Gina Marie. She wanted more out of life than babies and pasta, and she didn't care what the nun's had said about having babies. She wanted to enjoy life a little before having kids clinging to her legs, and losing her figure.

Mary Catherine wanted to live in a big house like those on Todt Hill in Staten Island where the wealthy went to live when they moved out of Brooklyn.

She drove by them whenever she and Carlo went for a Sunday drive together. The winding driveways, marble floors, and servants cleaning and cooking for her in a big Todt Hill house were her dream. But it is only a dream and she knew at that moment in time she needs to continue to work, and is willing to work hard to get ahead.

"So what if they were mob homes, what I don't know can't hurt me," she said to herself.

And if she ever did know she is smart enough to not say anything, to anybody.

Mary Catherin and Carlo's parents both chipped in together, and a large wedding is planned for the both of them. All the uncles, aunts, cousins and friends were invited.

Gina Marie, as the older married sister, is to be the matron of honor, and her kid sister Carmen is to be a bridesmaid.

Mary Catherin's gown is purchased in Bay Ridge. It is a beautiful white gown with some beading mid-waist. Her sisters and mother came to help her pick it out. Theresa Avila is elderly and isn't able to come that day. But they took a picture of Mary Catherin trying on the gown she selected, and they showed it to her when they had the film developed that week. But Theresa Avila never lived to see the wedding. She died shortly after the shopping trip.

The wedding ceremony went smoothly, and the whole family drove to Long Island for the celebration.

The two families decided to have it at a famous catering hall on Long Island that usually had four or five affairs going on at the same time. The hall is large enough to accommodate their large families, the price is reasonable, and a good time is sure to take place.

The wedding reception went off well.

Some of the male guests, if you looked very carefully, had small bulges under their suit jackets. It is not pockets full of cash, but gun holsters, filled.

Gina Marie looks good in a custom-made gown Rocco had her buy from a seamstress in Bensonhurst.

Carmen is the maid of honor and looks stunning. She also noticed some of Rocco's associates staring at her, and in a strange way, it excited her. The older the fellow is the more she enjoyed it. The younger guys she blew off, but she did dance with some of the men in their forties and fifties. They knew who she is so they minded their manners, and did not make any remarks to her, or try to arrange a date for another time. Everyone is well behaved that night.

Mary Catherine's wedding is uneventful and is a typically jovial affair. The band played, people danced, and everyone went home enjoying a good time.

***

A year after the wedding she and Carlo saved enough money to buy a small house in the Bay Ridge section of Brooklyn, only two blocks from the bay, off Shore Road.

It is a starter home with three small bedrooms, and a fenced in backyard. The stucco front of the house was in good condition and when you opened the windows you could smell the ocean air from the bay blowing in, as it was just a stone's throw away.

At night during warmer weather, you just opened the windows all over the house and the cool sea air felt great. Especially since Mary Catherine and Carlo did not sleep in pajamas.

Carlo works as a salesman for one of Paulie's construction companies and seems to be doing well. He is a smooth talker and makes friends easily. He has the rare ability to think on his feet and make a deal.

Paulie's cousin Gus was in a trade union as a labor leader, and he made the right connections with the building department. Whenever a permit was given out Gus knew about it and told Carlo.

Carlo, somehow, was able to find out what his competitors were bidding and he usually underbid them and is awarded the job.

Gus's contact in the building department would tell the architects they had to build in a lot of extra work safety precautions in every job. This was to prevent the unions from causing them problems such as work stoppages. That drove up the price of the building. But Carlo knew he did not have to do the extra work so he underbid his competition.

He didn't get every job he bid on. Carlo didn't even try to. He had more than enough to keep his crews busy. Plus he didn't want it to look fishy so he overbid on the medium and smaller size jobs. But on the bigger ones, he almost always won the contract.

"Carlo," Paulie told him one day, "Don't be greedy and stupid. Only go after the big jobs, and let the other guys feed on the smaller fish. That way they won't get too pissed off and do something stupid. Like, go to the District Attorney." Carlo understood and remembered what he is told.

Carlo is making good money now. Mary Catherine is starting to think of building her dream house on Staten Island. When she walks to the park overlooking the bay she can see Staten Island and the Verrazano Bridge. Her dream house is almost hers she would think to herself.

Once a month Rocco would stop by a construction site that Paulie is handling and visit him. He would walk into the trailer office, and pick up an envelope for Paulie. The union crews that work on all of Paulie's jobs are indebted to him for the work. The union local's president would arrange for a cash payment to be made for miscellaneous expenses and brought to the trailer for Rocco to pick up.

Rocco always brought some food for Carlo and himself to eat. They made it a point to meet at these sites so they could relax and talk freely.

Usually, he brought tuna and some fresh ham and cheese heroes made in a butcher shop near Mary Catherine's store, with freshly baked rolls, and six cans of Piel's Real Lager Beer. The crisp taste of that beer was their favorite, especially with a deli sandwich.

If it was nice weather they would often eat outside watching the building go up.

"Hey Carlo, I bought some sam-wiches. Do youse want tuner or ham?" Rocco would ask when he walked into the trailer. Carlo never understood why he would ask the same question every time. He always took the tuna, and Rocco always chose the ham. He just chalked it up to habit. Anyway, the sandwiches were fresh and tasty. Not like the crap they serve on the lunch trucks that always stopped by a construction site with soggy bread, and dark meat tuna fish with no taste.

What they had between them was very similar to a father-son relationship as Rocco was older now, and took Carlo under his wing. He liked the kid and thought he would go far in the construction business with him and Paulie. Carlo was not the type to do Rocco's job, yet. He was still learning the construction side of the business first.

To be a collector and enforcer, that would come later.

But through marriage and business, they were family.

Carlo was making very large deals for Paulie's construction company all over the city, and the money is flowing in. Through his contact with the building department, he is getting very good leads when a permit is applied for.

There are the box seats at Madison Square Garden for the Knicks and Rangers. It cost thousands for each game with free food and drinks included, but it is worth it.

The politicians and building department personnel are always taken to the "Garden" as were the union leaders. It is in the seclusion of the private box that cash could be exchanged for favors. Sometimes there would be a dozen people there, or just Carlo and a guest if private business deals had to be transacted. If someone needed some construction work on their home the arrangements were made in the box at the "Garden." Nobody left empty-handed.

Plus they get to see a game on top of everything else. They would get free tickets to a major league sport, free food, and cash. What else could a person on the take ask for?

In New York, the Knicks ruled, as did the Rangers. They had avid fans, and the Ranger fans are known to be fanatics. Just ask Dennis Marvinski who played for the Islanders. One year the Rangers were in contention to get into the playoffs and Marvinski hit the Rangers star player and broke his ankle. For years after that, even after he retired, whenever the Islanders played in Madison Square Garden the building shakes when the fans start chanting "Marvinski Sucks". People go to hear that chant from the fans.

If they are really big shots Carlo would hire a limo to take them safely home, especially if they are carrying a lot of cash after the game. He did not want them to lose it on the subway, or in a taxicab.

Another one of the head supervisors for the New York City Buildings Department is a frequent private guest at the Garden with Carlo. This is a very expensive guest but it is cheaper than getting building code violations and constant inspections. This allowed Paulie to use cheaper materials and concrete mixes on a major job. Plus there are no work stoppages to worry about due to building code violations.

The years passed, and eventually, Carlo and Mary Catherine bought a large house on Todt Hill and moved in. Everything is going great and it seems her dreams are being fulfilled.

She hired a big name interior designer from Manhattan and shopped with him at all the expensive showrooms in the D & D Building.

There are no red velvet sofas or dangling crystals in her home. Only high-end contemporary designer furniture and luxury appointments everywhere are in the home. She even bought a glass occasional chair, and red leather, imported, handmade sofa from Italy. Her home could have been in any home decorating book. It was magnificently stunning inside.

The front door to her custom built home was not to her liking so she installed a two-story high custom red mahogany. It is so massive, and expensive, the custom builder who built her home refused to install it. She needed to have the door manufacturer put it in.

There are two brass light fixtures that flanked her front door. Each cost five thousand dollars and the heated floors in the bedrooms also were preinstalled when the house was being built. This is a nice feature she wanted so when she hopped out of bed in the morning the floor was warm, and her feet would not be chilled.

The builder, as part of the package, installed a circular driveway with handcrafted red bricks individually placed into a pattern. No expense was spared for her dream home.

The house is situated near the highway and is close enough to the Verrazano Bridge she could drive over to Brooklyn quickly whenever she felt like it, and visit her mother Anna Marie and Carmen, or just go shopping on 86th street.

She didn't like the stores on Staten Island because she felt there is not enough of a quality selection like there is in Bensonhurst. Besides they do not discount if you paid in cash like they do in the old neighborhood.

But Brooklyn, and the construction business is changing.

***

In the Brighton Beach area of Brooklyn, the Russians had moved in and there is a very large population of immigrants living there now. The area is known locally, and to New Yorkers, as Little Odessa by the Sea.

They literally took over an area that was once made up primarily of Jewish families from Eastern Europe. The stores now have their signs in Russian and English, and all kinds of Russian specialty shops and cafes opened there. Although there is a large population of Russian Jews they do not affiliate with their faith, except to acknowledge it is "good blood." That is the result of seventy some years of Godless communism.

A few Russian nightclubs also opened in the area. Some of the nightclubs were on Brighton Beach Avenue, and some on Coney Island Avenue. With their red and gold décor, and the Czarist eagles flaunted all over the place they catered almost exclusively to a select group of clients.

And along with them came the Russian organized crime people.

They are even more ruthless than the Italians. Many of them served time in the Russian prison system and were hardened psychopathic criminals who withstood years of torture and deprivation.

So when Paulie decided to build a complex of three apartment buildings right off of Brighton Beach Avenue and underbid a Russian construction company, more than a few feathers were ruffled.

The week after the contract is signed one of Paulie's foreman is working on a job in Manhattan, he went to lunch, and never came back.

As the foreman started to cross the street to go to a donut shop for coffee a van pulled up next to him. He was in the crosswalk; two arms reached out from the side sliding door and dragged him into the van. They sped off with him in it, and he was gone in a flash.

His dead body was found the next day, bruised and dumped on a sidewalk, in the Gravesend section of Brooklyn with a copy of the contract that Paulie won stuffed in his mouth.

The war was on.

For the next few months, not too many people were killed or maimed on both sides. There was retaliation here or there but nothing massive. Nobody wanted the press or police to notice, so they were spaced out.

It also helped that each side was watching themselves more carefully, and were armed to the teeth. The men wore either light windbreakers or business suits with a small bump protruding from their sides. That was where they kept their guns, except for Olga.

***

Olga was an experienced KGB assassin from the old Soviet Union, and she now worked for the Russian mob. She is very tall, slim with long brown hair, and with red streaks in it. She dresses very stylishly in name brand clothes, and could easily be mistaken for a high fashion model.

She had a thin face, a muscular, toned body, and strikingly high cheekbones. Olga works out daily both running and weight lifting. The only difference between her and a Madison Avenue model is they both had killer looks, but Olga could really kill you.

Often she wore her holster under a flowing skirt, strapped to her upper leg. On the other side of the custom, holster was her trusty knife. There were no telltale bulges to be seen.

She would follow her target and get on a bus with her intended victim. Just before the target would get off she would step down into the bus's stairwell first in front of him, bend over, take out her gun, then turn, and shoot her victim once the door opened. In the mayhem and confusion, she would walk away. She never bothers to look back. She is an excellent marksman and rarely misses her shot.

Olga trained in Russia to use explosives as well as in hand to hand combat. She is extremely lethal and loyal to Viktor. He was her handler in the KGB, and also her lover.

A New York City detective, who was gathering information on the Russian mob in Brooklyn, was to be her target. She was instructed to take him out.

Olga called the detective and told him that there is a suitcase with documents that he would be very interested in having. He is to meet her in City Hall Park in Manhattan at noon. She told him she would be sitting on a bench, she was blond, and in reality a brunette.

He felt secure in meeting her there for many reasons. First, it was in a very public park with plenty of people walking around. Second, if there were gunshots the police that are stationed at City Hall would be within walking distance. And third she is a woman, and he had this macho attitude towards women that gave him a sense of confidence. The third reason was his undoing.

As he entered the park he is looking for a blond woman sitting with a suitcase and did not notice who was walking towards him as there are many people in the park that day.

Walking casually towards him Olga approached the detective slowly walking by, and purposely bumped into him. As they turned to face one another she said excuse me, and with her knife she made a quick thrust stabbing him forcefully in his chest as it slid effortlessly piercing his heart.

Not looking back she calmly kept walking as he fell to his knees with the knife protruding from his chest and collapsed in the middle of the park with hundreds of people around who saw nothing.

Chapter 7 -

Paulie is well aware of what is going on with all the killings in Brighton and knew this madness needs to stop. He is, above all, a pragmatist.

One night his construction trailer at the Brighton Beach site is firebombed. The flames had reached fifty feet into the air. The night watchman luckily decided that night he would leave the trailer, and stop watching television. He is on the other side of the complex walking his rounds when the explosion happened. That is what saved his life. Otherwise, he would be toast if he stayed in the trailer, and continued watching television.

The fire at the trailer is officially reported to be caused by an electrical short circuit that ignited blueprints on the floor. This is what the New York City marshal said caused it after his palm is greased. No one is killed and no major damage done so he took the bribe, walked away, and no police arson report is ever filed on the incident. This enabled Rocco put in an insurance claim which exceeded the actual damages by thousands of dollars after the claims inspector is also given some cash.

But Paulie knew better than to think it is an accident.

The heavy earth moving equipment is also sabotaged. Sand is put in the gas tank of the trucks and in the engine cylinders of the cranes. It is getting very expensive now.

Almost every day, early in the morning when they had to shape up, a construction worker didn't show up for work or quit. He would call in immediately after he saw his car was drenched in acid. They understood the message that is being sent.

They knew what is going on and didn't want to end up like the foreman did in Manhattan. The workers are well paid but their life is worth more so they often called out sick.

Knowing what is going on Paulie knew he had to settle things down, or he would start to lose big money.

He put a call into Viktor, and a meeting is set up to discuss things.

Finally, Paulie had Rocco meet with the Russian boss's brother, Dmitri, and a deal is to be made.

They met in a diner on Flatbush Avenue near Avenue U where they hashed out an agreement.

Dmitri came to the meeting with Olga at his side. She spoke perfect English without a trace of an accent. That was due to her KGB training as a spy and killer at the Kremlin.

Flatbush was considered a neutral area and they all felt somewhat secure being there. Carlo joined them for the meal also.

Rocco did most of the talking and Carlo just listened and approved by nodding his head.

"Look, Dmitri, les talk bout us jus get-tin tagether and mak-in this shit go away," said Rocco. It ain't good biz-niss an all we wan is ta make money," Rocco said over coffee.

"Vat doo yooo propoze" answered Dmitri.

"How bout we hire some guys you wan-ta get paid, and we share in the costs an profits," Rocco suggested.

Olga just sat there silently and listened. She also is looking around the diner, to be safe. She trusts no one.

"We also hire a Jewish accountant that we both agree on, and he decides who pays what, and how much profit there is" Carlo chimed in.

"Das sounds goot but I have to tahk to mine brudder" Dmitri answered. "I vill get back tooo you sooon".

They all left together and walked out to their cars. Rocco and Carlo went to Bensonhurst while Dmitri and Olga had their driver take them to Brighton.

The deal is sealed when Carlo receives a surprise visit one day from Dmitri as Carlo is walking to his car after work. He didn't see him approach and is startled when he tapped him on the shoulder. Olga is with him.

He saw her first and froze. He knew who she is and of her reputation. He thought he is going to get whacked.

"Carlo," Dmitri said, "it iz ah deal. Baht remember dat you are in my neighbor-hud and theengs could happen if you dahn't keep you bahr-gain".

Paulie would now have to hire men from the Russian construction company, and Viktor would share in the profits as a joint venture. The Russian construction crew never showed up, as agreed, but they were paid anyway. Paulie didn't care. It was the cost of doing business. He just cut corners and quality a little more. It is a miracle the building didn't collapse before it is finished.

Paulie also agreed he would not build again in that area of Brooklyn unless it was a joint venture with both of them as partners.

New York is a big city and the Russians, at this time, only wanted to keep their hooks in Brighton. Paulie had all five boroughs to work in any way so this is not a big deal at the moment.

To really help smooth things over Carlo is instructed by Paulie to meet with his Russian counterpart, Dmitri, and make nice over lunch. He is to get to know him better, as a defensive move for the future. It could not hurt.

Carlo is told to talk about some smaller future deals in the Brighton area to see how the suggestion might go over.

And maybe they would share some joint ventures in gambling and prostitution, and expand their holdings together as partners.

Carlo also wanted to see how far they could agree on things together. Someday in the future, a favor might be needed from either side. You never know.

They decided to meet at a neutral place, Younger's restaurant, on Flatbush Avenue just across from Brooklyn State University. The food is very good, tasty, and their desserts are fabulous.

Dmitri seemed to come alone, and he sat down with Carlo at a booth in the front. What Carlo did not see was Olga sitting in the rear of the restaurant looking at a menu. She was there as security for Dmitri, just in case.

Carlo ordered a delicious thick-cut prime rib au jus with roasted red potatoes and veggies, and Dmitri ordered a cheeseburger deluxe with raw onion on it with well-done fries. His breath stunk from the onions, but luckily Carlo did not sit that close to him. They sat across from each other at a table in the front.

The conversation is very general. They spoke about nothing in particular but did agree to meet again at the beach area in Brighton. They planned to walk to the water's edge, and with the waves lapping against the sand they could talk privately without fear of being overheard. The noise from the wind and the water makes it impossible to over hear what they would be talking about. Especially since it is fall, and nobody is sitting on the beach sunning themselves.

After finishing their food they sat and ordered Younger's famous cheesecake with fresh strawberries and coffee. Carlo had his with strawberries on top. Dmitri had his plain. They lingered a little while, digesting their meal, and then decided to leave.

They left together through the front door and walked outside onto Flatbush Avenue to take the subway home. It is early in the afternoon, the sun is shining brightly with a slight breeze, and they seemed to enjoy the weather and the walk. What a nice day to finally relax, and put a major headache behind them.

About a half block away or so Olga is following them discreetly and watching.

As they are walking along Fulton Street to the subway they are being closely tailed by three Jamaican Rastafarian types. They are between them and Olga. It didn't appear to be unusual as the area is mostly minorities, and the chaos of congestion is normal there.

Nobody noticed them due to the heavy pedestrian traffic on the avenue.

The noise from the trucks that are roaring by, and the diesel fumes from passing city buses blowing onto the sidewalk, seemed normal, and nothing is out of place.

As they took two steps down and started to enter the dark unlit entry into the subway system, they smelled the stench of urine coming up from the filthy and stained concrete steps.

The tiles on the walls had not been washed in years, and they were all marked up with graffiti. The entrance from the street to the subway is dank and dirty. Two Jamaican men were walking up the stairs as Carlo and Dmitri came down them.

The two Jamaican's stopped and pulled out their guns.

"Give us your money and watches," the lead Jamaican said to them, standing almost in their faces. Carlo and Dmitri stood frozen for a second.

"Take it easy," Carlo told him. "You can have whatever you want, just relax."

The three Jamaican men walking behind the two came closer. They stopped behind them and stood on the first step down into the subway. They then pulled out their guns and put the gun barrels right onto the back of Carlo and Dmitri's head.

Carlo and Dmitri felt the cold steel pressing into their heads and knew this was not a casual holdup. This also prevented Carlo and Dmitri from fleeing up the stairs and away from the two in front of them.

It was a staged holdup. The intent was not robbery, but to send a message.

The shots rang out and echoed throughout the stairwell walls.

In a hail of bullets both Carlo and Dmitri were left lying dead on the filthy concrete steps. Their slumped bodies fell with such force that they were thrown down the flight of stairs. Olga saw and heard everything that is happening, but she is too far away to stop it.

So many bullets entered the back of their heads that they literally distorted the front of their faces causing them to be unrecognizable. A small bag of cocaine is placed in each of their hands, to be found by the police.

They knew when the police investigated they would ask their families if they were doing cocaine. The message would then be sent back to Paulie, this is revenge.

Later when the police investigated no witnesses are willing to come forward and talk to the police. They didn't want to end up like those two did. The police couldn't find anyone that saw anything. Literally, hundreds of people were in the area at that moment but silence ruled.

Olga came running at the sound of the shots and saw the three men fleeing out of the subway entry in all directions. She was too late, the Jamaicans killed both men.

She knew those gunshot sounds very well. She lifted her skirt and took out her gun. She fired point blank into the chest of one of the men when he ran towards her as he was fleeing the scene. His body flew backward from the force of her bullets, and he fell down into the stairwell of the subway station, landing on top of Carlo.

The second man turned and ran into traffic. He saw that Olga had a gun and had just shot his buddy. He was dodging the speeding cars and trucks that are flying by him on all sides. The traffic light had turned green and the race was on. As he twisted and turned trying to get to the other side of a six-lane highway he is clipped by a passing truck. He spun around from the impact and is tossed into oncoming traffic, and hit again. Olga saw him lying there unable to move. She would deal with him later if he survived.

Olga stopped, then turned, and started to chase the last of the three Jamaicans as he ran the other way. He had no idea that someone was following him, and what was about to happen to him. He was too focused on getting some distance between himself, and the shooting.

He ran across Flatbush Avenue and walked briskly into Brooklyn State University, at their corner entrance. He ignored the security guard at the front desk

151

who politely asked for identification, and he kept walking with Olga not far behind. Olga saw him go into the building and quickly followed him in. She too ignored the call of the security guard to stop and show identification.

This building used to be the Ultimate Showcase Theater, and they converted it into a gym for the basketball team and classroom upstairs.

The shooter looked for the men's room to hide in, and also to wash his face and catch his breath.

Sweating heavily from the excitement, and with his heart beating very fast from adrenalin he desperately looked for the men's room. He had to hide, and take a moment to regroup his thoughts. He was only nineteen, and this was his first hit. The young man is extremely nervous about getting caught and gave no thought at all to killing a total stranger.

Finally, he saw the men's room door and ran in. He stopped in front of the sink, took a deep breath, and turned the faucet on.

As he bent over the sink to rinse his face with cold water Olga slowly walked into the men's room. She saw him bending over the sink.

She quickly ran over to him, took out her knife, and pressed it to his throat as she clutched his dreadlocks tightly. "Now I vant you to valk slowly into da handicapped toilet at da rear of da room" she ordered him in a forceful voice.

He was overpowered and surprised by her. He slowly went with Olga into the last stall. She was walking right behind him, their bodies touching, as she was still holding the blade of her knife tightly to his throat.

"Now get down on your knees an poot your hands behind your neck," she ordered him as she securely latched onto his braids, twisting them tightly around her left wrist.

"Who had you doo this?" she demanded.

He knew if he did not answer her he was a dead man.

"I have a wife and a kid," he cried to her. "Please, I did not do anything. You have the wrong man," he pleaded.

But she saw everything, and he was with them. There is no mercy in her heart, she never had any. What he did not know is that she is also a psychopathic killer, and carries no remorse or feelings for any of her victims, as was he.

Olga twisted his hair tighter, pushed his head into the toilet water, and held it there. He started to gurgle. Bubbles were coming up in the water. She continued to hold his head in the water as he trashed his feet.

She yanked his head up and again demanded to know who was behind the shooting. He was coughing and trying to take deep breaths of air.

He had enough. Out of breath and going limp from exhaustion, he told her. That was his undoing, and he knew it.

Once he told her who ordered the revenge hit, and where they came from, she had no further use for him. She cut forcefully into his jugular and pushed his head into the toilet like a chicken that was just slaughtered. She held it there underwater to muffle any sounds he might have made, until he stopped kicking and thrashing, and his body fell limp against the toilet.

Then she let go of his hair and cleaned off her knife on his shirt.

When she was satisfied that the knife is cleaned of blood she cut off a few of his dreadlocks, stood up, and turned to leave.

As she walked out of the handicapped stall a security officer from the university walked in. The front desk security guard had reported them entering the building and this security officer was investigating the unauthorized entry into the building.

"Please stay where you are," he ordered her. "What are you doing here in the men's bathroom?" he demanded.

"Just one second please," she said to him as took out her gun. She instinctively raised her arm and aimed at his heart, and she shot him in the chest. His body jumped back towards the wall and then dropped to the floor. Calmly she stepped over his sprawled out legs and walked out of the bathroom into the main hall. People are running all over the place taking cover where they could find it. They all knew what gunshot noise sounded like, and in the confusion she calmly turned to walk out the front entrance.

Once outside she crossed the street to see about the shooter that was run over. There are police cars and ambulances with their lights flashing, stopping traffic while they just stood there talking to one another. It was a crime scene, and it would be hours before they let traffic continue normally.

The body is covered with a sheet and this told Olga all that she needed to know about the shooter.

Newspaper and television reporters were already on the scene taking pictures for tomorrow's front page and the evening news reports. The New York Post and Daily News enjoyed a field day with the bodies in the subway stairwell, the body in the middle of Flatbush Avenue, and the two bodies in the men's room at Long Island University. Even the mayor went on television that night with a press conference vowing to see justice is served.

Placidly Olga stood at the curb, fitting in with the crowd, and waved down a taxi. She took the cab to Brighton Beach to report back to Viktor what happened.

She also brought back as a trophy the dreadlocks she cut off of the killer after he died. It is a trophy of sorts, and proof to Viktor that she killed him.

***

There is a new criminal element in Brooklyn now besides the Russians and Italians.

The Jamaican drug gangs wanted a piece of the action, and they are not shy about taking it.

They branched out from running numbers in the minority sections of the city and started to take over the prostitution business also. They are pushing out the independent pimps and madams. But they wanted more.

Cocaine is being imported into the country by the Jamaican gangs, from Mexico, in containers labeled with boxes of designer clothing. They would hide the drugs in the clothing boxes and take it out when they opened the containers in their warehouse in Bed-Sty. Then they would distribute it all over the city and New Jersey, primarily in urban areas. This is only going to be the beginning for them, is what caused the killing of Carlo and Dmitri.

Paulie had an informant who owed him money and is a union foreman in the dockworkers union at Port Newark. His crew knew in advance what was on the manifests before the containers reached the docks. It is not unusual for a container to fall and break open by "accident" and some of its contents stolen and fenced.

His contact had found out that a forty-foot container of big-name designer clothes was coming in

155

soon, and Pauli is interested in that sort of thing also. He had contacts on Canal Street in Manhattan to fence hot stuff for him in the back of the small Chinese shops along the street.

But this time Paulie wanted the whole container of designer clothing to sell through his network, not just partial contents that "fell out by accident".

He considered it diversification.

Paulie had Carlo arrange a heist of the trailer carrying the designer clothes container when it left the docks from Port Newark and drove to Brooklyn. They were after the clothes, to be sold later on the black market, not the drugs. They had no idea cocaine was in the trailer.

What they could not sell on Canal Street the street level guys would then fence. The designer clothes are sold at high schools after the kids come out from school, flea markets, or some stores on 86th street where they had their hooks in the businesses. Some of it would be sold in the pizza parlors that Paulie controlled all over the city. Or they would sell it, or trade it, at deep discounts to the hookers who worked for him.

When the tractor-trailer pulled out of Port Newark it is being followed. Rumbling over the Verrazano Bridge, carrying the container, it eventually drove off the highway at 95th street in Brooklyn, and stopped for a red light. A car directly in front of it and one behind the trailer also stopped.

They waited for the truck to drive a few blocks, and then they stopped the truck when it was on 3rd Avenue in the fifties under the elevated highway. Carlo stepped out of the front car, told the driver to walk away or else, and then they planned they would drive off with the truck and container.

Beanball climbed into the cab and started to drive to their warehouse in Red Hook. If anyone is in his way and tried to stop him he is prepared to run them over, and keep going.

He eventually turned onto a rutted side street immediately before the Gowanus Canal and went a few blocks to an old steel gated brick building. There is a lot of graffiti written all over it with garbage and old tires strewn across the street.

Beanball stopped in front of the gates, and the truck's air horn blasted two short bursts. Someone walked out of the side door to see who it is. Recognizing Beanball they went back in and pulled the steel gate up which allowed him to drive in the building.

Carlo arrived there ahead of him and is waiting with a crew of Latinos to unload it.

Walking over to the container he took wire cutters and cut off the seal. Slowly he opened the container doors and latched them on the outside. Then waiting for him to tell them to begin, in the warehouse in Red Hook, is his Spanish crew. He told them to begin unloading the cardboard boxes and place them unopened by the side cinderblock wall.

He started to open some boxes himself. Suddenly he froze. He was stunned to find millions of dollars in cocaine hidden between the clothing inside. He stopped opening the boxes and just stood there for a moment, thinking.

Rocco knew, when he was told, someone big is behind this imported container because it costs huge sums of money to pay the bribes, and to also import that much stuff. This is a major haul, not a corner dealer type of shakedown.

Carlo closed the boxes he opened and took them into the small office in the rear of the warehouse. He locked the door, then called Rocco, and told him that it is urgent he come to the warehouse immediately.

Rocco came down to see for himself. Carlo also told the helpers again "do not open any more boxes just stack them by the side of the warehouse."

Then Carlo said to Beanball "tonight take this truck, and dump it far away from here. I don't want it found near this warehouse. And don't forget to wipe the steering wheel and doors. I don't want any fingerprints found on it."

Late that night Beanball drove the truck after it was unloaded and took it to Queens. One of the other guys took a car and followed behind him. He would then take him back when the truck parked.

He left it in an industrial section of Queens almost in the shadow of Citi Fields, near some closed junkyards. Most of the buildings there are empty and shuttered. It is an ideal place to leave it. Months might go by before anyone noticed it is parked. All the police will do is continually ticket it until finally someone calls and complains about it being there for months and not moved.

"Carlo," Rocco said when he arrived, "I think youse jus ripped off duh Jamaicans. I heard dey are bring-in dis stuff. Dis is a lot of shit here".

He heard from his street crews that the Jamaicans are importing coke, and he assumed they just ripped them off in a big way. As it turned out he was right. There would be repercussions if they ever found out who did it.

Carlo needed help distributing this much stuff, and he farmed it out to the other families crews in the city. It is Paulie's idea, to spread the wealth, not get greedy, and tick someone off. He even cut the Russians in on it. There was that much cocaine. But he kept the designer clothing for his crews.

The many crew captains needed take the cocaine home and hide it themselves. It is too dangerous to keep too much cocaine in one place. Carlo and Rocco know exactly who took what, and the guys knew better than to screw with Rocco and Paulie. They hid it in their basements if they owned a house or in their closets if they didn't. This month Red Hook and Bensonhurst were overflowing with cocaine stashes.

One cousin of Carlos also put bricks of marijuana in his basement. It is a virtual drug warehouse, and Chris's mother had no idea what is being stored in her basement. She never goes down there. If she only knew there are hundreds of thousands of dollars of illegal drugs sitting downstairs she would die.

The Jamaicans finally put two and two together with the help of a street dealer who is frozen out of the drug deal by Carlo. His supplier told him he couldn't get any good stuff for him because it was going to made guys first. Then if he had the right connection, and there is some left over, he would be given some coke to sell. This is how the Jamaican drug gang found out Carlo is involved and hijacked their cocaine shipment.

They began to track him down. They knew he was in construction with Paulie's crew, and they started to go to every construction site in Brooklyn.

They would have one of their men go into the trailer office looking for a job. It took time and they didn't let up until they found him.

It was too big a heist to ignore.

Someone had to pay for it.

When they finally were able to isolate him on the subway steps, in their home turf no less, Dmitri is an innocent bystander who was in the wrong place at the wrong time.

But they didn't know who Dmitri is or care. His older brother Viktor is the boss of the Russian mob, and revenge is to be extracted. The Russians are now involved and are looking also for them.

A new drug war is about to begin.

***

Shots are fired and both men fell onto the subway steps. Carlo & Dmitri were shot in the head three times and Dmitri is also shot in the chest. They died instantly. Slowly their blood is oozing out onto the subway concrete floor, mixing with the urine from the night before.

The shooters put their guns away and ran. Three ran out of the subway and onto Flatbush Avenue. The two coming up the stairs ran back into the subway station and jumped onto the first train that arrived. It didn't matter where it was going. They only went one stop and then walked off, and waved down a gypsy cab to take them home to Springfield Gardens, Queens.

But Olga had found out who they were, and where they hung out. As the tide marks the pier the end of their lives would come, and very soon.

***

Carlo is killed, and Mary Catherine is now a widow.

The wake is held at the Fattachie Family Funeral home in Bensonhurst. The burgundy and brass décor seems very high class, and the crosses on the walls are 24-carat gold plated.

The coffin is brass and chrome plated with a huge golden brass cross on the top of it. The handles are chrome with brass accents, and the pure white sateen inside is never seen.   The casket is perched on a slightly raised platform, and a kneeling bench placed in front of it for people to say a prayer for him.

Mary Catherine sat there for two days in front of the casket.

Dressed in the required black dress and veil she sat and quietly met with visitors.

She received condolences from the people who came to see Carlo off. Some she knew, some she didn't. They were from all walks of life, and most of them worked for Carlo in construction.

The men who came in with bulges under their suit jackets were Rocco's associates or Paulie's.

There were flowers all over the room. The walls could barely be seen, and they kept coming. Finally, they had to put flowers in another room so people could come in, see Mary Catherine, and give their respects.

Her two sons, Anthony and Frank, are there also. They are in their late teens by now and they sat close to their mother to comfort her.

Rocco came over and sat down next to Mary Catherine.

"Lis'n, I spoke to Paulie and he is go-in to see dat youse are taken care of," Rocco said in a very low voice so no one else could hear him. "I am go-in to stop by now an den drops off some cash for youse ta live on. I miss him. He was like a kid brudder to me."

Rocco is devastated, as he enjoyed a close relationship with Carlo, like an older brother, and genuinely cared for him. Carlo was more than a brother in law to Rocco.

"An d'own worry bout da boyz. I am go-in ta look afta dem also. Dey will be okay. I promise" Rocco said to Mary Catherine.

His wife Gina Marie is sitting on the other side of Rocco. She wiped her tears away with a tissue

161

and looked at the coffin. It is a beautiful casket that cost Paulie over ten thousand dollars. The white sateen inside is never seen as they closed the casket. The Undertaker could not hide the damage the bullets did to Carlo's face so they decided to keep the casket closed.

There are beautiful flowers set all around the coffin.

People are kneeling on the footstool in front of it, crossing themselves and saying prayers. This went on for two days almost nonstop.

Gina Marie bent forward and put her hand out to comfort Mary Catherine. "We'z are fam'ly," she said. "We will be deer for youse d'own worry," Gina Marie said trying to hold back her grief as she spoke.

Carmen is sitting across the room just staring at her sisters. She couldn't believe what is going on. This confirmed to her that she would never be with someone who is "involved." It is too heartbreaking when it comes to an end, of course, assuming you actually loved him.

Mary Catherine is dressed in the obligatory black dress and flanked by her two boys. Her two sons are wearing black pinstripe suits with large gold crosses hanging out on top of their shirts.

As a courtesy, Viktor and Olga paid a condolence call at the wake, as Rocco and Paulie did to Dmitri's funeral the day before.

It is a little surreal when the Russians walked into the funeral parlor. They looked more like gangsters than the homegrown gangsters who are sitting there. But peace is made, and now they are brothers in grief.

All of Paulie's crews came to pay their respects, as did members of the other New York and New Jersey families. Even Paulie's good friend from Philadelphia came with a small crew of guys to pay their respects. They did it for Paulie.

There were three black Cadillac flower cars leading the procession to the cemetery.

Carlo was very well liked and respected. Being Rocco's brother in law didn't hurt either.

A few days later, after all the funerals are over, Paulie called Dmitri's older brother Viktor in Brighton. They both decided, after a short coded conversation, to go on a quick overnight vacation together to Atlantic City.

Viktor had hired a limo to drive them down to Atlantic City. Olga sat in the front with the driver.

They enjoyed the ride together but spoke very little in the car. They are waiting to get there before they could really talk without feeling the FBI is recording their conversations. This is why they wanted to stay at a hotel on the boardwalk. They felt they could walk and talk after dinner, and not worry they are being listened to. The sound of the waves coming in from the Atlantic at night muffles any eavesdropping on them.

They gambled, had dinner together, and made sure they are seen all night in the casino, on the hotel's security cameras.

For dinner, they went to The Steak House at the casino and ate a delicious meal.

As an appetizer, Paulie had the fried calamari and Viktor ordered the blue point oysters. For the entre, Paulie ate the ribeye steak they are famous for, and Viktor had the roasted prime rib of beef, au jus.

They each had three side dishes and were surprised the whole dinner is compt. It seems Paulie's friend from Philly was told they are coming, and he took care of it for them.

They stayed at the casino and had a good time there during the evening. Paulie's friend from Philly also sent over some escorts later in the evening to keep him company, and warm, at night. Of course, Viktor had Olga with him.

The next morning the New York news media are ablaze with a report of a few Rastafarian men killed in Queens. They are reputed to be Jamaican drug gang members. No details are given out to the news media so it is reported it is a gruesome killing.

The bodies are found in the basement of a rundown apartment building in Springfield Gardens, Queens. Their hands are tied behind their backs, their mouths stuffed with socks to muffle any sounds, and their eyes were pulled out of their sockets. It is so vicious that their necks are slashed to the point where they are almost beheaded.

There were other atrocities to the lower parts of the body but the police did not let that news out to the media. They might have a need for that information in the future and did not want the world to read about it.

The coroner's office determined before they were killed they were tortured and their bodies mutilated. Then they were killed.

The killers wanted to be sure that someone would understand all actions have to be accounted for, one way or another. A strong message is being sent.

It had all the markings of a revenge killing, but the Russian and Italian mob didn't do it.

It was contracted out to the Cuban guys from Union City, New Jersey. They are even more vicious than the Russians.

It seems Paulie's cousin, who is a union big shot on the docks in Port Newark, personally made the arrangements.

If it were only one person the Cubans would have just picked him up off the street. They are known to pull their car up next to someone, get out, and two or three men grab the victim. They literally throw him in the car and drive away. After abusing him for a while they'd cut him up, and drop the body parts in the Meadowlands for the fish, birds, and other animals to finish the job. He would never be found. That is what the Cubans usually did.

This time there were too many bodies to dump so they just left the Jamaicans in the basement to rot.

The bodies were found in the morning by an elderly tenant who is also the super. He discovered the bodies when he went to check the boiler room to make sure the pressure in the furnace is correct, and the heat would go on.

When he walked into the boiler room there was so much coagulated blood that his shoes stuck to the floor. There must have been over an inch of blood on the cement basement floor.

The Cubans hired one of their Jamaican prostitutes to lure a Jamaican gang member they had a name of to come down into the basement. She had his phone number and called him. The hooker said that she "was sent by someone you know, and all expenses are paid for in full. I am outside and am not sure which apartment house you are in. Can you come down and get me."

When he came down she took him into the boiler room where he was jumped and beaten. He was told to call upstairs, and tell them to come down, and join in. Then he was killed. One by one his friends came down to join the party. They met the same fate.

It is a trap and they all fell into it. But they were only part of the gang. The top boss of the drug gang is not there. He went on a date that night and was out of the building.

He escaped because he was with some white blond that he had been seeing. He now needs to avenge this killing. He knew who did this. He would not forget.

***

Mary Catherine owned almost everything she ever wanted. Luxury cars in the driveway, a big house on Todt Hill, expensive furniture, two sons, but her husband is now dead and buried.

After a short period of grieving, she decided that she must get on with her life as she is still relatively young.

Mary Catherine refused to wear the traditional black dresses that her mother and grandmother wore after their husbands died. After the funeral, she was finished wearing black. She is more modern than they are, and a lot younger when her husband died.

She didn't work for many years, and Carlo left her very well off. Plus her brother in law Rocco is keeping her in the lifestyle she is used to.

Mary Catherine felt she needed to do something for herself, and get out of the house. Time passed, and she knew she must go do something, anything, and move on.

It is very lonely at night in the house. She is getting depressed sitting around with no one to talk to, in a huge house, in the middle of nowhere. She thought maybe if she lived in Brooklyn, or Manhattan, she could always go for a walk or shop on the avenue. She felt she needs to move out of Staten Island for her sanity.

Mary Catherine called a local realtor who was recommended to her by a neighbor, and she put her house up for sale. She had the requisite Todd Hill marble and curved stairway leading up to the two-story high mahogany front door. The manicured lawn and water fountain sat in the middle of a circular driveway. Glitz was the word best used to describe the house. Both inside and out it was done up in Bensonhurst Baroque.

She had thought of moving back to Bensonhurst, but she decided she really wanted to live somewhere in Manhattan.

New York has a lot of apartment condos for sale, and she liked going to the city with Carlo on the weekends to see plays and museums. He tolerated them, but she was creative and enjoyed them immensely.

She was not brought up in an artsy or cultured household, but she liked what she saw in the city, and began to learn to appreciate the arts. Plus she always was somewhat artistic and enjoyed drawing when she was younger.

It took about six months until the right person came along to buy her home. The buyer was a Russian couple from Brooklyn that heard about it from Viktor.

Nobody knew it but Viktor was the actual buyer. He used one of his men to buy it from her, and nobody knew about it. This is his way of tipping his hat to Carlo. Plus Olga liked the house very much and wanted to live there.

After she sold her home she hired some Russian moving company that Rocco suggested she use. They moved her to the upper east side of Manhattan, on East 83rd Street between 2nd and 3rd Avenue, and then she started to look for employment to keep busy. Part-time is all she was looking for.

There is more culture in Manhattan than in Brooklyn, and she enjoyed living in that neighborhood.

She enjoyed the small shops and walking on 3rd Avenue and seeing all the people.

The Metropolitan Museum of Art is not too far away, and she often walked there. The exhibits are great, and she also enjoyed relaxing in Central Park.

Rocco had a friend of a friend who owned a used furniture store in Greenwich Village, and another on Fourth Avenue. People thought he was selling antiques because he made sure it had wormholes and other markings on the wood. But what they didn't know is that he put them there.

He had arranged for her to get a job in the used furniture store as a saleswoman. She did not know anything about selling furniture but she had a few years' experience selling general merchandise on 86th street when she was younger and single. And she had a flair for color.

The owner, Irwin Kapowitz, agreed to train her and teach her the business. He knew of Rocco and who Rocco worked for. His friend had told him to watch what he said and did with this new sales girl. She is related to Rocco, and he is not a person to screw around with.

Irwin retired from the Western Union Telegraph Company and started this business with his girlfriend at that time, Patricia.

Patricia knew the used furniture business and taught it to him. Their first store, a small one, was on Fourth Avenue in Manhattan, and it did very well. The window was full of armoires with chicken wire where the glass would be. Old walnut chairs were scattered around and the aisles were very narrow. It smelled old and musty like an antique shop would. The traffic whizzed by on the street and the modern era was just outside his door.

Irwin even purchased two genuine Tiffany lamps he bought very cheaply at tag sales in Manhattan. The people had no idea what their value was, but he did.

Irwin and Patricia started to live together and the money rolled in. She now wore Gucci, Pucci and other expensive designer brands.

With the new found money he is making in his Greenwich Village shop he bought a loft building, and moved in with her. He told her he is renting there but in actuality he owned it. She never knew.

But Irwin had a roving eye, and one day Patricia came home to their apartment and found him in bed with one of her girlfriends. He jumped out of bed and ran over to her to try and explain what was going on.

He knew he was caught, and it was hopeless, but he tried anyway.

His words stumbled out of his mouth and made no sense.

She saw what she saw and nothing he could say would change that. Patricia yelled at him and would have none of it.

She grabbed a suitcase, packed her jewelry and clothes as best she could. Then she stormed out slamming the door behind her and never returned.

Patricia is fuming while she was walking away. Then she saw his motorcycle parked on the sidewalk near the loft building and pushed it over. "Screw him," she said to herself, and then she continued to calmly walk away, and out of his life.

By this time he owned two successful stores and needed help. Patricia managed one store, and he did the other one. Now he needed a manager for the Fourth Avenue store.

His store in Greenwich Village is in the basement of a thirty five-story apartment building.

It is not unusual for a building to have shops on the ground floor. Irwin installed two huge vats of a volatile chemical stripper in the back warehouse area which he used to strip the finishes off of the used furniture. Then he would refinish the wood so it looked really old but in great condition. If there were mirrors on the front doors of an armoire he would take them off, cut them down to be wood rimmed mirrored trays, and then install chicken wire on the doors in its place.

The trays were just extra income he could generate from the cabinets. They looked great because the mirrors were old, the silver veins were showing, and they sold for a lot of money.

The problem was that those stripping chemicals were highly flammable and combustible and could explode and set the high-rise on fire if they ignited.

But he had an ironclad lease and at that time there is nothing the landlord could do to get him out of the building. The landlord's fire insurance is immensely high due to this risk. Irwin obtained a certificate of occupancy for the store, and he is not going anywhere for the next fifteen years.

The fire codes back then were kind of lax, and the building inspectors always took a bribe anyway. This is where Paulie's connection in the building department came in handy. Irwin's friend is a cousin to one of Rocco's men. The fix is made, and he received his certificate of occupancy so he could do business there.

With his girlfriend leaving he needed someone to cover the Fourth Avenue store. He is on the phone calling the Village Voice to place a help wanted ad when this tall lithesome blond walked in looking for a job.

Irwin said he would hire her, but she would have to sleep with him. She agreed, but only if he married her first.

This is how Irwin married his second wife, Rose.

She was introduced to his family and friends, and they had a nice life together. He was kind and very generous to her.

Unfortunately for Rose, a few years later, she found herself in the same position as Patricia. Except for this time Irwin is not dating Rose as a girlfriend but is married to her. And Rose, his wife, took half of his property and goods. His girlfriend Patricia, a few years before, had left him for the same reason but walked away with nothing. His financial situation is vastly different now.

So Irwin needed to start over again almost from scratch with his remaining two stores in the city.

He almost lost the Fourth Avenue store to Rose in the divorce, but Rocco helped him out by speaking to her one day when she was in the shop alone.

As Rocco entered the shop two of his larger men stood in the doorway. One fellow was looking out to the street, the other glaring in at Rose. She sensed what is happening but stood still, and waited for Rocco to approach her. She had no idea who he is or what he wanted. But she felt something bad is about to happen.

He walked slowly over to her.

Rocco is very soft spoken and did not yell or threaten her. In his best Brooklyn English he explained to her that his friend "Irwin has a financial prob-lem" and he, Rocco, "thought dat maybe youse could help Irwin out."

171

She just looked in disbelief at his serious face, and then to the two men standing in the doorway. She understood what he is saying without his having to say anything further.

"Okay" was all she had to say.

Rocco turned and left quietly.

The second he was out the door Rose picked up the phone and called her divorce lawyer. She told her lawyer "I want nothing more from Irwin but a divorce" in a firm tone. "I have his money, let him keep the business. I want a divorce," she said again.

Her divorce lawyer is a real feminist bitch, and did not understand what is going on, and tried to talk her out of doing this. "Irwin has some really good assets in the business, and Rose, you are entitled to half of them, if not more," she told her on the phone. But she did not succeed in her changing her mind. "No, I want nothing more. And I mean it" Rose said to her. She is adamant about this, and finally just hung up the phone on her lawyer. There is no way she is going to start up with the mob.

Rose put on her coat, took her pocketbook from the shelf behind the counter, and emptied whatever cash was left in the register, and put it in her pocket. She walked to the front of the store, opened the front door, turned to lock it, and left.

And she went away quietly after that back into the ocean of humanity that Manhattan is, never to be heard from again.

Irwin's business is slowly growing again when Mary Catherine was brought on board to help out, selling to the customers and running the Fourth Avenue shop for him.

Her outgoing personality and wit is an asset to the business. She is a charmer. She let her light brown hair grow long, and put some red streaks into highlight it. The boots and tight-fitting jeans she always wore were stunning on her with her hourglass shape. She fit right in with the type of hip customer Irwin is catering to in that store. Mary Catherine could talk to them on their level, and she was a success selling for him.

Irwin is aware of her background from his friend and didn't immediately ask her to marry him or sleep with him. He knew better.

Mary Catherine is in her early forties now, and Irwin is only a few years older.

They hit it off and became good working friends. It is an easy, casual, working relationship.

Often Irwin would leave the Greenwich Village store, and bring in lunch for her, or buy her a bunch of flowers for her desk as a surprise before her store opened. He was truly smitten by her strong good looks and her easy personality.

They started to go out often after work for dinner and soon they found they were very fond of each other. Both could sit for hours and talk and laugh and they usually lost track of time when they were together.

Irwin never had this experience before.

It was usually only for sex he dated women, but Mary Catherine is different. He did not dare to touch her, yet.

Irwin knew if it went any further he couldn't fool around with other women. Stupid he wasn't. She was Rocco's sister-in-law, and he knew of Rocco, and what he did for a living.

But he was very smitten by her, and she knew it.

Unlike the other girls before her, Mary Catherine had as good a personality as they did, but she had a backup in Rocco that the others did not have.

She had plenty of cash from Carlo hidden away in a vault in Brooklyn under an assumed name and identity. A few years before Carlo died he had fake United States Passports made for each of them, and their sons using false names, just in case. He felt if they had to flee the country they would be able to. He kept assets hidden under these false names in the Caribbean in various offshore banks.

Mary Catherine liked Irwin very much, and she offered to buy into his business to help him expand. She was crazy for him as he is both handsome, educated, and did not make a play for her like other men would have. She thought he is different than the others, and he was.

And he was also well spoken.

Irwin didn't have the "Brooklyn" accent that almost everyone from her old neighborhood had. He didn't have the dees, dems and doe's that are the essence of the Brooklyn dialect.

He hesitated at first dating her. But Mary Catherine had other ideas.

One night while they were out to dinner she asked him "would you like to grow the business a little faster?"

"Of course I would" he answered. "But that requires a lot of money to advertise, and buy some better goods. At this time I don't have it".

"Well I do" Mary Catherine answered. "I have some money put away for a rainy day I can lend to you for the business."

Irwin is not keen on getting involved with the mob in any way what-so-ever, except for one.

"Tell you what," Irwin said in a calm voice, putting his hand out and gently grasping her hand, "There is only one way I can accept your offer."

Mary Catherine instantly knew what he was about to say, and she smiled and looked directly into his eyes, waiting for the next sentence.

"We have been working together… for a while now" he slowly spits out the words. "And I have come to really appreciate you… and respect you"…he paused to gather his thoughts before going on. "Mary Catherine… will you marry me?" he asked her just as the waiter was bringing their coffee.

She was not expecting that tonight, but the conversation had flowed directly into the question, and she was very happy to hear it.

"Of course I will," she answered. She was thrilled that he finally moved their relationship forward. He had been the perfect gentleman since they met. And she thought it is because he had manners, and respect for her; not knowing it was the fear of Rocco instead.

Irwin then stood up and leaned over the table and kissed her for the first time.

He knew that Rocco would protect him if he married his sister in law. Or at least that is what he thought. If he took her money and not marry her he would be in deep trouble if the business did not flourish. Irwin also knew that his days of fooling around with other women were over, or he would be too.

But Irwin, to his own disbelief, was genuinely in love with her and they both agreed to get married even if he was Jewish and she Catholic.

Mary Catherine thought back to her high school days when she dated Sam. Her mother had her break it off because he was Jewish. But now she was older and independent and could marry whomever she wanted to.

She had cast off the heavy yoke of religion altogether that had bound her somewhat loosely in her youth. Her heart told her to marry Irwin and she was going to.

They were not about to have any children at this stage of their life so the religion issue didn't bother either of them. If truth be told they were both not observant in their faith anymore, and it just did not matter to them.

Religious intermarriage was now okay. Gays were openly coming out of the closet and living with each other, and proclaiming their love and wanting to get married. Some even had gone to Europe to get married, but it was not recognized in the United States yet. Even civil unions were not yet recognized by a lot of states.

Her family already knew Irwin as they met him a few times when Mary Catherine brought him to family functions. There was peace in the family and they all liked him, including Rocco. For some strange reason, those two men hit it off and had a good time when together at family functions.

On a Monday morning which they selected as their day off they didn't open the shops themselves but had their workers do it for them. The two of them took the subway downtown from the village to city hall and went to get a marriage license.

After they paid for their license and had their blood tests done at the clinic down the block, they went to city hall to set a date to be married.

One week later they were married in a civil ceremony at city hall. None of their extended family was there as they wanted to keep it very private and fast. But everyone knew it was coming. Only her sisters and family were present.

Mary Catherine was radiant as a bride again and she was smiling from ear to ear. Gina Marie was the matron of honor and Carmen was the maid of honor. Mary Catherine's two sons were there also and Anna Marie came too, with Carmen, to witness it.

Everyone was happy and cheered when they were pronounced husband and wife.

They honeymooned in Times Square at a small boutique hotel and had dinner at Carmelo's. After dinner they went to see a play and then back to their honeymoon suite, and the next day they went back to work.

With the influx of her money, their business thrived and grew larger.

Mary Catherine if finally at peace with her life.

But her two sons would be another thing altogether.

Chapter 8 -

It is about noon when the phone rang in the Fourth Avenue store. Frank, Mary Catherine's youngest son, was on the phone.

"Ma, Anthony and I were just arrested, and we need a lawyer," he told her matter of factly. There was a slightly perceptible plea in his voice.

He and his brother Anthony were just arrested by the FBI.

They are alleged to have stolen jewelry which was in a secure holding area at Kennedy International Airport, and the FBI had it on videotape.

This is a federal felony, and they needed bail and a lawyer, quickly.

Mary Catherine knew who to call. Not a lawyer just yet, she had to get the right one. So she called her brother-in-law Rocco for the name of a lawyer.

She knew in her heart that somehow he was behind this. It is his way of taking care of Carlo's boys. Getting them to work for one of his crews is Rocco's idea of taking care of the boys, just like he did for Carlo.

Rocco recommended a Jewish lawyer by the name of Jonathan Gootman.

Gootman is the guy to go to when someone in the "family" needed a criminal defense lawyer. That was all he did.

It is common knowledge in Bensonhurst if you wanted a lawyer or doctor you had to go to a Jewish one. They were the best. And Jonathan is the one they went to. He had connections.

***

For over thirty-five years all of Jonathan Gootman's clients are believed to be innocent until proven otherwise. It is rare that it didn't turn out well.

Sometimes a plea bargain is the only way out of a long prison term, but it is an approved plea bargain. Not only did the prosecutor have to approve it, but a higher up in the "family" had to approve it also.

This is only necessary when someone couldn't be bribed or "persuaded" not to testify. In a worst-case scenario, they would just disappear. But only if the case involved a person higher up the ladder, and they could find him.

Witness protection became a hurdle the mob had a hard time overcoming; especially if a new identity is provided and they are moved across the country somewhere. The Feds did that a lot but the New York prosecutors just tried to hide them away in a hotel somewhere.

When the "family" finally approved a plea deal, arrangements were made for the defendant's wife and children to be taken care of while he was in prison. It always happened that way, always.

The girlfriends were left out to dry. If they were capable of causing a problem, by talking to the district attorney, someone would be sent to explain the facts of life to them. That always worked too.

Gootman once had a client who was at home one evening when the doorbell rang. He was served with a federal summons to appear in court for a large investigation by the FBI into a bank's illegal loans. The guy knew better than to testify. The moment he was handed the summons, without even looking at it, he grabbed his heart, fell to the floor, and was immediately taken to a private hospital to be under the care of a specially selected doctor.

He stayed in the hospital under his doctor's medical advice, and Arthur's legal advice, until the summons expired.

Six months later he was discharged and sent home.

One day his doorbell rang and a summons was once again served to him. Immediately he grabbed his chest, fell to the floor, and was again admitted to the hospital with a heart attack. This went on three times until the prosecutor finally decided he did not need him. There was no way this guy was going to testify, and live to tell about it.

***

That afternoon Jonathan Gootman met with the two boys in Manhattan and was told by each of them, individually, that they made a wrong turn off the Belt Parkway, and were looking for someone to just give them directions back to the highway.

It was just an accidental turn, a wrong turn, they said that caused them ending up in a freight terminal at the airport. When they stepped out of their car they found this box lying on the floor with no one around. So they took it for safekeeping and were going to bring it to the supervisor on duty to return it.

They had no idea the box contained uncut diamonds imported from Amsterdam. It was consigned to a famous diamond importer in Manhattan.

This was their story to Gootman, and they were smart enough not to talk to the FBI until their lawyer came to see them. They told the FBI nothing, based on their lawyer's advice.

The next day Arthur relayed the story to Rocco, and the wheels were set in motion. Rocco acted as if he had no knowledge of anything and did not say anything to Gootman.

Gootman told Rocco when the boys went back into their car the FBI stopped them at the exit to the hanger and arrested them for theft and a few other sundry federal felonies.

They were innocent victims, good Samaritans, trying to do the right thing…they had explained to Gootman.

Rocco arranged for their bail and they were released on $500,000 cash or bond. Rocco quickly posted it for them.

About a week or so later the federal prosecutor dropped the main charges.

The diamond importer said he forgot to tell the police that he had asked the boys to pick up a box for him at the airport. He was not willing to press charges.

It seems that when the importer went to the garage under his office to get his car, at the end of the day, two men stopped him as he was unlocking the door, and convinced him it might be unsafe to drive home in this weather. "You never know when lightning can strike a home or car," they explained to him. "Maybe you can do the right thing about the boys?" This was their favorite thing to say, and it always worked too.

He looked at the two men and suddenly realized what they were saying, and about whom.

They continued "we can put a lightning rod on your house for you at no cost. A person always needs protection. And it also protects your car too" they concluded.

The importer was an older Jewish man with gray hair and slightly hunched over as he walked with his cane. After being in the diamond business for over forty years he had met all types of people, including gangster types. He immediately knew what they were saying as they towered over him. They spoke with authority in their voice. No nonsense, just plain talk.

One was in his face and the other stood two feet behind him. They did not smile. Just spoke matter of factly and calmly to him.

He had his diamonds back so what the hell, he thought to himself. The next day he called his lawyer.

"Leo, this is Max. About that federal case with the two boys...I do not want to press charges against them" he told him on the phone. "Tell the prosecutor I am not going after them."

"Why the hell not, Max? They were caught red-handed with the diamonds by the feds. Screw them. Teach those momzers a lesson" he replied.

"Leo, listen to me. There are some things I cannot talk about, and this is one of them. Drop the charges, okay, goodbye."

Not understanding why Max wanted to drop the charges Leo called him again and asked him why he changed his mind, but Max refused to give him an answer.

Max just said "it is the right thing to do...for me and my family".

When he said that, then Leo knew someone threatened him, so at that point, he did not press Max for any more answers.

The only charges that did stick were a trespassing charge, and the boys were let off with a fine and probation by a Federal judge in Brooklyn.

It seems that Jonathan Gootman did his magic again, with some help. The judge's law clerk's brother owed some money to one of Paulie's bookies, and a conversation was started with the brother. A debt could be forgiven if the judge was very lenient with the boys. So the law clerk tilted the conversation with his judge to let them off with a slap on the hand.

***

The boys now had to move out of Staten Island after their mother, Mary Catherine, sold her house on Staten Island. With the help of a realtor they purchased a condo together in Brooklyn Heights. They shared the two-bedroom condo apartment in the Heights and also bought all their furniture from that furniture store on Coney Island Avenue near Avenue N in Brooklyn.

The Heights is a rejuvenated area with restored brownstones all over the place. For young men with money, it is the place to live. Their condo is on the second floor with 10-foot ceilings and wood moldings all over the place. It was built at the turn of the century, is very spacious, and in a very desirable location. Only a few short blocks away is the subway and in the other direction is the plaza overlooking lower New York Harbor.

Anthony is on the reserved side, laid back and gentle. He often went with the flow and definitely was a follower and not a leader. Quiet would be a more apt description of him.

Frank is just the opposite. He is more like his mother, lively, talkative and has a way with words. He is also very focused on what he wants and rarely gave up on a goal he set for himself.

Park Slope replaced New York's Greenwich Village for many people because it cost less money to rent or buy, but it still was not cheap. It is just cheaper, and now very hip to live in.

Anthony met this girl one night at a club in the city, and they started to dance, drink and kiss. The club is dark but she stood out with her highly teased hair and her big smile and chest.

He took her home to his apartment after they left the club that night, and soon they are going out on a steady basis.

Her name is Basha and she grew up in Williamsburg, in Brooklyn. It is a very Polish area, and she went to an all-girls Polish parochial school where they taught both in Polish and English.

When the Pope visited Brooklyn he stopped at her school and church in Williamsburg. The Pope stood on the steps of the church and gave a blessing to all who came to see him. Basha's mother was there holding a few gold crosses in her hands wanting them to be blessed by the Pope. Afterwards, she gave one to Basha, and she never took it off.

Basha is a blond heavyset girl. Not fat, but plump, and had a nice gentle outgoing personality. Her clothes are nice enough but she always wore a bra that was one size too big, so she bounced around when she walked. She still lives with her parents, and they feed six cats that roam all over the house. They also adopted a few stray cats and neutered them.

Once, a mature stray cat that they had taken in was already pregnant, so they advertised in the local newspaper for free kittens once they were old enough to be separated from the mother. They felt it was not the Christian thing to have them put to sleep. They believed that all life is sacred, even animals have a soul.

They received a telephone call one night from a church in Brooklyn that wanted a kitten. The church encountered a minor problem with field mice and hoped the cat would solve it, as it grew older and larger.

The next day Basha put one of the kittens in a small cage and hopped in her car to take it to the priest that had called her. Her car was a mess, with old newspapers, empty beer cans; wrappers strewn about and generally had a disheveled look inside.

Basha drove the kitten out to the church to give it to Father Brian, the priest who had called. She had a little trouble finding his office, but she eventually was successful. He is a very charming man, and they sat and talked for hours.

Father Brian, as he liked to be called, named the kitten Stash. It is a Polish name for Stanly, after Basha's father, who had a heart attack a few years before but survived. Father Brian did this after talking to Basha for a while in his office.

Being heavyset Basha didn't have a lot of boyfriends, although she was bubbly and friendly.

As the conversation wore on Father Brian realized that Basha is a very lonely person, as was he, and he decided he would try to take advantage of the situation.

Before long she and the priest are having an ongoing intimate relationship. Every week she would drive out to see him. She felt sorry for him being alone and offered him comfort in a way that he was not supposed to be having, or enjoying.

She would go into his quarters and undress him. Their encounters were not long, maybe fifteen minutes. He was usually in a hurry and did not want anyone to hear them. Then he would sneak her out the back door.

Basha felt wanted.

She also started to have an on again off again relationship with a Jamaican boy named Hamilton that she had met on the subway. They were both packed in like sardines at rush hour and a conversation was started as they were jostled together with the train's back and forth movements. Her large chest was heaved tightly against his, and she gave him a small smile. He realized that she is coming on to him.

He thought she is cute and he liked heavier girls, especially if they were white. And she thought he had a very nice physique. That also was not lost on her. So they exchanged phone numbers before they exited off the train, and they had a long conversation on the phone that very night. Before long they were meeting at various motels and became sexually intimate.

But her mother went nuts when she found out she was dating a black man. So Basha would sneak out of the house and see him once or twice a week after work. Whenever he wanted her, it was on again. The comfort he gave her satisfied her longing to be wanted, both physically and mentally.

The priest did the same thing. He would call her when he wanted to see her, and he also took advantage of her need to be loved and wanted.

She just couldn't say no. It was not in her vocabulary.

Basha worked in Manhattan for a high-end salon cutting and styling hair and she did very well with her tips. She always dressed nicely and stylishly even if she was on the chubby side. She felt there is no excuse not to be fashionable.

Anthony was smitten with her from the first time he saw her. After only a few dates he thought of marrying her sometime in the future. He never saw her weight, just her personality, and went head over heels for her. Plus the sex was good too.

They started to date on a continuous basis. Anthony thought it was an exclusive arrangement and Basha never told him that she was still seeing the priest and Calvin.

By now Anthony was working for his Uncle Rocco doing office work for one of the construction companies. He would drive to the site and take care of whatever paperwork there was to do.

Frank also had a girlfriend, or two, or three.

He preferred to play the field and had a penchant for Black and Spanish girls. He liked them shapely with long flowing hair and big chests.

Frank was on an errand one day for Rocco. He had to go an office building in Manhattan to deliver an envelope to Paulie's lawyer.

It was in midtown and he had to take the subway to 34th street and Broadway. When Frank arrived at the building he walked in and was looking at the directory in the lobby for the law firm of Kapoya, Mench, and O'Neal. They were on the thirty-second floor and he took the elevator up from the marble lined lobby.

When he walked off the elevator he saw two glass doors that went from the floor to the ceiling with the firm's name acid etched on it. He slowly opened the door and walked into the waiting area. The elegant carpet and wallpaper stood out. This is an expensive law firm.

Then he saw this stunning Puerto Rican receptionist, Juanita, sitting at the front desk. She was older than him, in her early or mid-thirties, and breathtakingly beautiful.

It was hard to tell her age just looking at her, but she has an aura about her of sensuality that attracted men. She wore tight-fitting clothes that outlined her sensuous body but was not revealing, yet she still looked professional. She is perfect for a front desk position in a busy law practice where she is to answer the phones and greet any clients coming into the office.

***

Juanita used to in a shelter until fairly recently.

Her mother is a crack addict and she had no father that she knew about.

Finally, after a few years, she walked out of her mother's apartment as a very young girl and took to walking around the city, and prostitution. She was homeless and used to walk the streets looking for handouts and any odd jobs she could find. Juanita tried to save her money for the future, and when she felt she could afford to leave the streets, she did.

When she saved enough she moved into a women's shelter in Brooklyn to get her life on track. They gave her a small room to share with three other girls. It was warm and there was free food in the lunchroom. Juanita is not stupid, just driven to survive, by any means that she could.

When Frank approached the desk he said he had "a letter for Mr. Kapoya." She looked at him, smiled, and said she would bring it to him if he left it on the side of her desk. Frank put it down where she asked, and then started to chat with her. It was small talk, nothing serious, and both of them laughed and hit it off right away.

He is a charmer and a real smooth talker.

Juanita is very attractive with her long flowing black hair, and her dangling gold hoop earrings, contrasting with her caramel toned, Latino skin color.

Frank went back to the desk and they continued their quiet conversation. Then he leaned forward on her desk, and asked her "when do you get a lunch break? I would like to take you to lunch today, what do you say?"

Looking up at him she saw a very cute young man and figured why not. It was a free lunch, and he spoke very nicely to her.

"Okay, I get off at twelve-thirty, meet me downstairs in the lobby" she answered him.

Later when she walked off the elevator he is waiting there for her, and they went to a small restaurant located nearby.

It is the usual Manhattan coffee shop with burgers cooking on the flattop and fries boiling away in greasy oil. But they always tasted so good.

During lunch, they had some more meaningless conversation about the weather and such.

"So how long have you been working there?" Frank asked.

The waiter interrupted her before she could answer, and asked for their order.

"I'll have a grilled cheese with bacon," Frank answered. "And I'll have the burger deluxe, well done, please," Juanita said.

After the waiter left she told him "I have been here for nine months, and I really enjoy it. The money is good, and they treat me very nicely. They are all lawyers and wait until I tell you what they did for us at Christmas time" she continued.

But Frank is not really interested in her company's Christmas stuff he faked real interest, and just listened to her.

"They took the whole company out to dinner at an Italian restaurant in the village. The average meal was over thirty dollars, plus they had unlimited wine for every table. It cost them almost twenty thousand dollars," she told him. "I thought it was very nice but crazy. I would never pay for something like that," she continued.

"Tell me," he asked cutting her off politely. "Are you seeing anybody or anything like that?"

"No not now, I did have a boyfriend for a while but I am single and living alone" she answered.

"You know, you are very pretty," Frank told her. "I really dig you," he said as he reached over to her holding her hand, and brought her toward him for a kiss.

She responded with a passionate kiss that comes from experience. This is not her first rodeo, in a manner of speaking.

Juanita really thought he is very handsome and did not think of his age. She is in her mid-thirties, and he was twenty-one.

Frank has his mother's good looks and a slender build like his late father.

The pheromones were kicking in on both of them.

After they finished lunch Frank said to her "let's go somewhere we can be alone for a while. Do you know anyplace around here?"

"There is an empty office on the floor below my company's. They are rehabbing the entire floor and the partners in my firm are planning to move their executive offices downstairs," she answered.

"Follow me and we can get off a floor below and walk up. I have a key to the exit door so we can go in" Juanita said.

They finished their lunch and both of them walked to her office building and took the elevator to a floor just below the empty one. They exited the elevator and walked around a corner to the fire door and walked up one flight. As they walked up the stairs he followed her, all the while he was looking at her toned legs; trying to peek up her short skirt. And she knew what he was looking at so she walked slower than she normally would have. The fact that she never wore underwear, only a thong, made it even more sensual for her, and later for him.

Her key worked and they went into an empty office that had some furniture in it. The walls were paneled in expensive rosewood and there was an expensive custom leather sofa bed at the end of the room, opposite a huge black ebony wood desk. In a few weeks, the finishing touches would be done and that floor would be fully occupied. But right now it was a temporary love nest for the two of them.

Frank pulled the bed out from the sofa and tore off the shipping plastic.

She hiked up her skirt to her waist and sat down on the edge of the bed. They finished their lunch in each other's embrace, and more.

Frank chased anything in a skirt. But there is something about Juanita that intrigued him, and he wanted to see more of her.

He made sure to write down her phone number so he could call her when he went home that night.

Juanita soon became a fixture at his apartment in Brooklyn, and the brothers often went on double dates.

They would go to the movies, out to eat or to a club in Manhattan to dance. Then they would go back to the apartment, and fool around in their separate bedrooms.

Finally, the boys tired of driving the girls' home in the morning, and they asked their girlfriends to move in with them.

But the apartment is not large enough for the four of them.

Frank is now making more money than his brother so he leased an apartment nearby. Juanita moved in with him, while Basha moved out of her mother's house, and moved in with Anthony in his condo.

During the weekdays when Anthony was at work, and Basha had her day off, she would go to church to service the priest. She did this on the days she was off from work at the salon, usually a Tuesday. This was a steady thing as she thought the priest is very handsome, but he would never leave the church to marry her. Besides she had Anthony and Calvin also. In her mind, it is safe sex with no strings attached, except pleasure. She had a very high libido.

The priest always had Stahsh on his lap, or nearby, when she came into his office. He was very appreciative of the cat and took good care of it. If he was busy that day and couldn't meet with her, she would call and meet Hamilton, her Jamaican boyfriend, at a motel near Kennedy Airport for a few hours of fun. Or at his house in Springfield Gardens, Queens.

Anthony had been hired by his Uncle Rocco to do paperwork in one of Paulie's construction offices. He is bright, worked well with numbers, and is very focused on his work; he never slouched off and is also very punctual.

Paulie then made him a fixture in his main office and put him permanently on the company payroll. He is competent on the work he did, and besides, he is Rocco's nephew.

Frank, on the other hand, is outgoing and very personable. He is promoted to become a "sales" trainee under the guidance of a trusted employee of Paulie named Sal. Frank is being groomed to take up where Carlo left off, in more ways than one. That is how Frank and Anthony became involved with the Kennedy Airport fiasco.

Rocco set it up with one of his crew members who worked at the Kennedy Airport terminal to have the bag accidentally drop off the baggage truck at just the right time. Frank and Anthony were to stop in, and pick it up and drive out with it. They were given directions on how to get in unnoticed through the gate. But things didn't work out as planned.

As time went on Rocco began feeling his age and wanted to take it a little bit easier. But Paulie was talking about retiring to Boca Raton and wanted Rocco to run things when he was sunning himself in Florida.

Rocco thought he could have Frank eventually move into his old job collecting so he began to personally tutor him on "things".

Frank is a quick learner.

Although he is living with Juanita he knew better than to talk business with her or bring her to family functions. He took her just about anywhere else and was proud to show her off. But not right now, to his family. They still had some old world views that Italians marry Italians and were prejudiced towards minorities, especially Puerto Ricans, and blacks.

They were not married, and Frank knew a wife could not testify against her husband. So until that happened, if ever, he said nothing to her about his activities with Rocco. At this time in his life, he enjoyed her company, her sexuality, but was not thinking long term with her. He felt he still had some wild oats to sow.

And Juanita knew not to ask too many questions. She had a feeling what he was doing for work. But having met those men in a brothel when she was much younger she didn't dare ask any questions. She knew how they were and what they were capable of so she kept her mouth shut. She is treated right and she is going to make the most of it as long as it lasted.

Juanita knew the type of guy Frank is, and she definitely is not making any long-term plans with him at this time either.

One night when Frank was out on business the phone rang. It was a call from Rocco for Frank. She answered the phone as she usually did when he was out. Rocco didn't identify himself to her but was very excited and wanted to talk to Frank. She didn't know who it is but told him Frank is out. Rocco wanted to get a message to him. He told her to tell Frank it was Hamilton. That was it. It was a very cryptic message.

Frank is collecting for Rocco that night and had to personally speak to a deadbeat in the back of a pizza parlor in Flatbush. Jimmy the Basket is with him and Frank did not have to do anything but talk. Frank is not a muscle guy, he was too small, but Jimmy is. Jimmy is a senior citizen by now, but still worked out and is very fit. He went to the gym every day for at least two hours. So the three of them walked into the back of the pizza parlor, and Frank asked for the three thousand dollars that are owed to Paulie.

The shop owner said he did not have it, he only had a thousand. Frank took that money, told him next week he will be back for five thousand, and had Jimmy take the man out back for a lesson in bookkeeping.

As Jimmy and the owner walked out the rear door Frank walked to the front counter and ordered a slice of pizza and a soda from a Spanish kid that worked the counter.

Once, Jimmy, the Basket was out back with the shop owner he grabbed him by his shirt and slammed him into the wall. Then he raised his leg and kneed him in the groin. The man fell to the ground in excruciating pain. Jimmy just looked at him and said,

"I'll be back next week" and calmly walked back inside and joined Frank for a slice or two of pizza.

That night when Frank came home Juanita awoke to tell him that someone had called and said to tell him "it was Hamilton".

She had no idea what it meant and did not want to know either. Juanita would not dare question him. It is business, she thought.

Frank couldn't get over the loss of his father, and how it drove his mother into the arms of another man. He liked Irwin, and it didn't matter to him that she is very happy and at peace. He wanted revenge. He wanted to find the money guy who is behind his father's death.

Now he knew.

Chapter 9 –

Growing up in South Philly is not the easiest place to mature. He had his share of fistfights, although he was also an altar boy. Brian Donovan was a good kid in a tough neighborhood.

His mother, Grace Ann, was very religious, and the family went to church every day, and not only on Sundays. They were a fixture every morning for mass until he entered into school and couldn't go in the mornings with her. But the boy's parochial school he went to always had services in the morning and students were mandated to attend. The nuns made sure of that.

At night when his father Matthew came home from working at a local factory, Grace made sure his meals were always on the table waiting for him. They were hot and tasty and she always made sure that there was fresh rye bread from the local bakery for him.

When she was younger she had worked in a ladies shoe store running back to the stock room and bringing out the selections that the customers request. She had the energy then to do that kind of work. But once she was married Matthew felt that as the husband he had to provide for his wife, and he would not allow her to work. He is the man of the house, and everyone in it knew it also. So Grace became a voracious reader and escaped her dreary life in books from the library.

Grace was a loving wife, took care of the house and the kids. She had four boys and Brian was the youngest. He was her last baby and she fawned over him. He could do no wrong in her eyes.

As a young bride she had a nice curvy figure, but after four children and a lot of cooking and tasting, she had put on a few pounds. Her cotton dresses were bought in the church's thrift store, and on occasion, the family had to survive on the goodness of Catholic Charities to sustain them.

But it is now in the past. As soon as Matthew received a position as foreman in the factory, and he started to make some decent money, she was able to buy her clothes in regular stores. But John Wanamaker's on Market Street in Philadelphia is too high priced for her. She could only walk through the aisles and dream.

After her last child, Brian was born the doctors had told her that there is some medical condition, and she should not have any more children or it would be life-threatening. She went to her local parish priest with her husband seeking a dispensation. Grace found talking about sex, and babies, to the male priest was very embarrassing to her. She was raised in a strict Catholic home where that kind of talk is never spoken. Yet she had to overcome her inhibitions in order for the priest to get the Bishop's approval.

It took a while but a dispensation from the bishop is eventually given for her to use birth control.

Brian's older brothers were a mixed bunch, and their interests and ways were very different from Brian's.

They were a mixture of street toughs and some were nerds. But they all were friendly and helped each other out if it was ever needed.

Brian liked order in his life. Chaos disturbed him, and often times his brothers were an unruly gaggle of young men until their father came home. Then they were as silent and respectful as anyone would desire in their children. It seemed that only he had their full respect and attention, and fear.

On his way home from work Matthew always stopped by the neighborhood tavern, McCrery's, for a beer or two with his buddies. They would watch the Phillies or talk about world events. They always had an opinion, thanks to the beer. It was rare when they would drink something stronger. Beer is cheaper and it allowed them to linger longer with their bar buddies.

The bar is not kept up very well, it is a typical neighborhood watering hole where they sat at the bar and killed some time. There is no need for ambiance. Just beer and a bathroom are all this crowd needs.

The place is dark, a line of stools at the long bar, a few tables, and chairs against the side wall. The jukebox would play when someone had the urge to throw a few quarters into it. Then Sinatra or Peggy Lee would sing their hearts out while the guys sat and had a cold beer or three from the tap.

Every once in a while Tess, the owner's wife, would cook something special upstairs and bring it down for the guys to buy. Her specialty is beef stew with plenty of meat, carrots, and onions in delicious homemade brown gravy. Her mother taught her how to make it in Ireland, and she also baked buttered biscuits to go with it. They always enjoyed it and left a generous tip as their way of saying thanks.

Matthew rarely ate there, as he knew Grace had already prepared dinner for him, and he did not want to upset her by not eating it. He always was very conscious of her feelings and loved and respected her. He never used offensive language when she was around and he did whatever he could for her.

They were an incongruous bunch of guys at the bar, but they were drinking buddies. Over the years they all became friends, and often would help each another's kid get a job, or car, or something. It didn't matter. They were there for each other. This went on for years and years.

New patrons to the bar were let into the group all the time if they became regulars. The only way to drop out was to be ill or die. And that started to happen more often than not, as they grew older.

When Matthew was finished drinking his two beers or so, and talking, he would then walk home the remaining few blocks for dinner. Somehow he was never late when he came through the door and saw his wife and family. His inner clock always worked fine.

He never was never drunk in public although he could get tipsy now and then. But he was good-natured and everyone liked him. Some people thought he might have kissed the Blarney Stone at some time in his life. Mathew was born and bred in Philadelphia and never left it until he was drafted into the army. He passed this gift of gab to his youngest and fourth son Brian, who also was never at a loss for the right words.

The fourth brother, Brian, was also very athletic and played in all the major sports that his parochial high school had. Baseball, track, football, and swimming were his strong sports interests. He did well academically and won a scholarship to a Catholic college.

Like his older brothers, he is a handsome boy, and they were all popular with the girls. But unlike them, he continued to go to church and hang out with the priests if he didn't have a date.

Every morning he would go to church with his mother. More and more he found comfort in being in church. It relaxed him, and he found there was no pressure on him when he prayed.

The priests often spoke to him about joining the priesthood, and at some point, he doesn't remember when he felt he would like to become a priest. He thought about it for a long time, and then he made a decision.

He filled out an application to a seminary and was accepted after an interview. His family sent him to a local college, and after he finished he was in training to be a priest.

Later he became a transitional deacon and eventually, he took his final vows as a priest when the Bishop called him.

He was sent to a small church in Queens, New York, as an assistant priest and was transferred eventually to a larger parish in Brooklyn.

Father Donovan stayed in Queens for a few years. It was there he learned how to be active as a priest in a parish's community life.

Brian made himself available whenever anyone called and wanted to talk to a priest. The church is near the Nassau County border, and it has a very large minority congregation. It was there he met Rayisha Jones who is the church's secretary.

She aided the priests in their correspondence and also helped out with the bookkeeping for the church. For a few dollars more she also helped clean the church and the private apartments of the two priests. In reality, she did everything that had to be done in a very small church. And she did it well.

Rayisha is a single mother of three children, and the salary she received helped her make ends meet. She is a big woman with a huge personality to match her considerable size. She wore a 22-size dress and jeans that were skintight. Rayisha is allowed to bring her two kids to the church after school, and they would all have dinner with the priests. It is very much like a family atmosphere. Maybe too much like a family in more ways than one.

Her goal is to become a nurse, and she is taking college courses part-time in the evenings and summers.

To help her get a college degree in nursing the church paid for her college tuition as a part of her salary. Strange as it seems no one at the church knew of this arrangement, not even the priests.

It seems the accountant for the diocese had an extremely "close" relationship with her. When he came on the days that the priests were out either at a parishioner's home or hospital visit, she would take him into one of the priest's apartments and sleep with him there.

He did not really look very hard at the books, he did not have to. He knew where the money is going.

It did not hurt that he is able to do money transfers from their bank account into hers. And that is why he never said anything about the funds being given to Rayisha.

And the new young priest, Father Brian, also is "extremely friendly" with her, although he never knew anything about the money.

"Father Brian," she said to him one day, "can I practice my neck muscle relaxation therapies on you that I learned in school"?

So he sat down on a kitchen chair and she walked behind him and started to massage the back of his neck while pressing her large, full chest into his back. That was all Father Brian needed as encouragement. Then she bent over and started to lick the back of his neck. He said nothing.

He turned around in his seat and started to kiss her. When he stood and cleared off the top of the kitchen table she needed some help hoping up on the top of it. Then she lay back on the table with her thick legs dangling.

It did not take him very long for it to be over. He greatly enjoyed his moment with her and this began a continuing series of encounters every week.

When they would meet in the hallway, if nobody was around, they would slip into an office. This went on for a while until the Bishop hired a new accounting firm after the old accountant died suddenly.

The new auditor came in and looked very carefully at the accounting records.

Rayisha was immediately fired, Father Brian was transferred to Brooklyn, and the elderly priest was retired the following week when a new head priest was sent to the Queens church. The bishop cleaned house as fast as he could.

***

In Brooklyn Father, Brian would become very active helping people with their problems, and was welcomed by the community. It was mostly Italians who made up the congregation, but there were some Irish and Polish also, but not many.

He made it a point to visit the sick at home and try to comfort them.

Often he would make a hospital visit of a congregant if he was informed of where they were. Father Brian put himself out for his flock, and was respected and admired by all who knew him. He was a good priest and earned the respect of everyone who came to talk to him.

If you had a problem and needed something to help you it was made known anonymously in the parish bulletin that was published every week. This enabled people to donate an article of clothing, or whatever it was, through the church and help out someone else.

Father Brian would also meet with you privately, later that week, in his office and try to help you out by talking about your problems. He did not want anyone to feel alone with nowhere to turn for guidance.

His calendar was almost always fully booked with people seeking his advice and counsel. He felt it was part of his calling to help others in any way that he could. And he was very empathetic to them.

He did the early mass every day and gave the older priest, Father Gianni, a rest as he was much older and getting frail.

Often he would go to the parish elementary school in the mornings and help out there when he could.

In the high school, he often counseled the boys when they were in trouble with the police or had problems at home. He really was very good at listening, and getting to the real heart of the problem.

This went on for years until he started to question his calling for the priesthood. He had put Rayisha out of his mind when he had come to Brooklyn. This was to be a clean start for him.

Then he started to have real doubts again.

Feelings that he had suppressed for many years started to bear down on him, and he had a hard time controlling them.

This is when he met Basha.

She had brought him a kitten, and they had named Stash. The intent on getting the kitten was to control the field mice, and then Basha started to have an affair with Father Brian.

He went to thank her for the kitten and she impulsively stepped forward to hug him. He put his arms around her gently as she pressed her chest against him, she looked up at him, and she kissed him on his lips.

In a moment of passion, he held onto her and lost control of his emotions and firmly kissed her back.

He started to rub his hands over her back, then lower, and eventually all over her body. They both lied down on the sofa in his office.

He stopped to get up and lock the door to his office, then turned and resumed a passionate embrace stooping over her on the sofa.

It was not along encounter, as encounters go, but it was very satisfying to both of them. He thought of it as helping her cope with life, and she did it to help relieve his stress.

Once a week like clockwork she came to him to relieve his stress.

Basha is a big blond with a few extra pounds on her. She felt sorry for the priest and felt this is her way to make a priest happy. She knew it is wrong but she enjoyed the sex, and so did he.

When she was younger she also helped a monk at a retreat in New York State relieve his loneliness in a similar way. She would drive to see him at night and service him. This was her way of serving the church.

Father Brian had no training other than that of a priest. He never thought if he should ever leave the priesthood he would be able to survive on his own. The church became his crutch in life, and he was not about to let go of it.

To his way of thinking he had the best thing going. Food, shelter, and Basha, and a little spending money were all he needed. If there were other expenses either a parishioner or one of his brothers would give him the money he needed.

Finally one day Basha met a young man named Anthony who was thinking of marrying her. She gave it a lot of thought and told Father Brian that she could no longer meet him continually. Maybe once in a while, but she would call him when she felt she was able to.

That was how their sinful affair ended.

Chapter 11 –

Carmen walked into the priest's office and sat down in the faded, crinkled brown leather chair that was in front of Father Donovan's desk.

Father Donovan gently leaned over his desk and took her hand to console her and ease her nerves. It was clearly visible that she is not relaxed. He did this many times before with many parishioners. But this time he too had butterflies in his stomach. There is something about Carmen which touched him in a way the others did not. Her innocent young face and feminine demeanor reached out to him.

She is about to tell her parish priest and confidant the darkest secrets of her marriage.

A small furry cat silently slid up next to her leg and rubbed against it. She picked it up, put it on her knee, and petted it. The cat started to purr and lay still on her lap.

"I guess Stash likes you," said Father Donovan. "He is a gift from a young girl I helped a few months ago. He keeps the field mice out of here."

Between his deep masculine voice and the warm comfort of the cat on her lap, she started to talk about her troubled marriage.

She had met her husband Nick a few years ago in a boutique in Soho in Lower Manhattan. It was only a block or so from Houston Street and it was starting to become the new hip fashion area of New York City. Carmen was shopping there with her girlfriend Nicole, and he was working as a custom clothes designer and stylist in the store.

He manufactured a small lineup of men and women's clothing which he designed and had them made in Chinatown specifically for him. Nick was told of this small workroom off Canal Street, and he went there to meet the owner, Mr. Lew.

It was located on the third floor of a loft building, and he could see the history of the building as the different paints and signs had faded into yesterday.

As he walked up to the third floor he opened the door to a small office and was greeted by an older Chinese woman. He introduced himself and then he was led into a small windowless office where Mr. Lew sat.

Sitting behind a large dark desk stacked high with papers teetering on the edge of collapse he leaned back in his office chair and lit a cigarette.

There are three phones surrounding him, and a teletype machine sitting in the corner. He pointed to the machine and said he uses this to buy and sell goods from all over the world. This is before the Internet made them obsolete.

"Right now I just bought some silk from India and sold it to a clothing company in Italy," he told Nick, trying to impress him.

It worked.

"I need a local workroom to do some custom clothes for me," he told Mr. Lew.

"I can do it…no problem" he answered Nick. "I have workrooms all over Manhattan and Brooklyn. I only need a few days to make whatever you need. And the quality is good" he boasted.

"Come look here" he called to Nick as he opened a door to a large workroom next to his office.

There Nick saw almost forty Chinese women sitting at sewing machines with piles of dresses and blouses piled high on the floor. Behind them, he saw three pressers getting the wrinkles out and two men hanging them and placing bags over them to protect them from soiling.

"If you really need large quantities I can get it made from Thailand," he told him as they stood there watching the people work.

A large fan was whirring above the steamers trying to keep them cool while young boys were running around gathering the finished pieces of clothing from the women sewing instead of going to school.

"I will bring you some of my designs tomorrow and I would like to see a sample made of them," Nick told him.

"Okay, no problem. Bring them to me about noontime. I will be back in the shop then" Mr. Lew said.

Nick thanked him, walked out and excitingly hurried back to Soho to the boutique. He felt he is about to make a name for himself and become a famous designer. He had confidence in his designs.

The boutique originally was a consignment store that a group of young F.I.T. students started a few years ago, and they used it as a showcase for their designs until they were hopefully well known. Once established they still continued to maintain it financially.

Nick is tall, thin and there is a sense of flair about him. He seemed almost gay, but not yet there. He is well put together in a fashion sense, but that is to be expected.

He usually wore an oversized shirt with a few buttons open at the top, jeans, and a wide leather belt with a buckle encrusted with crystals. If you had to give it a fashion name it could be called gay flash.

Carmen and Nicole shopped there often, liked his designs, and they went to try his newest things on. And on occasion, they even bought some of them.

Usually, they would hang out and flirt with Nick, and Nicole would invite him into the dressing room with them, against Carmen's weak protests. But nothing exciting ever happened.

When he did walk into the dressing area Nicole would start to kiss him and run her hands all over his body. Especially down his pants. Carmen would then have told her to stop it, and give her a chance. Finally, he would have to zip up the dress that she was trying on and ask them to leave him alone for a minute or so. On the surface, it appeared to be just good-natured sexual teasing. But both girls really liked him. Nicole did it for fun, Carmen for love.

Nicole worked part-time at a catering hall in Brooklyn, and she met a lot of men that way. She especially hit pay dirt when they had a private men's club stripper party. The tips and dates were awesome.

It was not unusual for her to go out with the young men she met there. They would take her to expensive restaurants and almost always buy her gifts if they seemed to really like her. And Nicole treated her dates very well with the feminine assets she had.

***

Nicole and Carmen met in high school and were bffs.

They went everywhere together and were extremely close, as they aged. It was to the point if you wanted to find Nicole just look for Carmen, and vice versa.

Nicole is a little shorter than Carmen and wore her jet-black hair teased high into the air. She only wore high heels that stretched her calves, and tight clothes that accentuated her figure.

Carmen is the more conservative dresser of the pair. Although she liked nice clothes she is not an extrovert like Nicole.

One day in high school, when they both were sixteen, they had a sleepover at Nicole's house.

It was a hot summer day and they had gone jogging along the bay at the foot of the Verrazano Bridge. There is a footpath that hugs the shoreline with a fantastic view of the ships coming into New York Harbor. The ocean ships coming into port, being escorted by the small working tugboats, were often passing by.

After the run, they went back to Nicole's house to shower.

Carmen went into the bathroom first to take a shower and refresh herself. She undressed and hung her clothes on the hook that was attached to the back of the door.

Nicole was also very sweaty. She did not ask if she could just step into the shower for a moment to quickly wash off. She told her.

"Carmen, I am just going to join you for a quick shower. I can't stand all the sweat on me"; she told her above the noise of the running water coming out of the showerhead.

When she stepped into the shower Carmen stood there and looked at her. It was not a large shower stall but a small bathtub with a showerhead over it. It was a very tight fit for both of them.

They were both in the shower together for the first time, and then they kissed lightly. After the kiss, they giggled.

The water was running down on their bodies as they embraced. They felt each other's flesh on their own and they had these feelings for each other that they never expressed before. This is the beginning of a long, special friendship.

That summer they became more than just good friends, in the biblical sense. This went on for years and never stopped. It lasted a lifetime between them, even as they entered old age.

They shared everything with each other, clothes, records, but not boyfriends. They still liked to date boys and would call each other at night after a date to tell what happened, if anything. Years ago they both decided they were bisexual, and that was that. No big deal, they thought.

So when Carmen continued to see Nick at the Soho shop she always was flirting with him, and when he finally asked her out on a date, she accepted.

She really thought he is kind of cute. He always dressed very sharply and is well spoken.

They went to fashion sponsored dinner one evening in the city, and they talked all night about everything. Not the small talk they had in the shop for a minute or two.

Carmen is a quiet girl, sort of reserved, and Nick always sought out the limelight. They were a classical ying and yang couple. They just fit together perfectly.

She introduced him to her older sister Mary Catherine one day while they were out on a date in Greenwich Village. They met her and Irwin for dinner at an Italian restaurant off of Washington Square, and it was a very pleasant evening.

Before going to the restaurant they decided to walk around Washington Square, in the Greenwich Village area of Manhattan. It is like a circus sideshow. They saw all kinds of people, all shapes and sizes, and colors.

They sat relaxed holding hands on a bench, under a large tree and watched the parade of people walk by. After a while, they looked at their watches. It is getting late so they stood, went to the restaurant to meet her sister, and sat down for a great dinner.

The food is terrific. Carmen had grilled shrimp with risotto and Nick order the breaded veal in a Masala sauce with roasted wild mushrooms and browned white potatoes.

The tables are packed together so tightly it is impossible not to hear the next table's conversation over yours. It just made the dinner more enjoyable to hear other people's private conversations.

They all ate the same desert; fresh skinned pears soaked in brandy and set afire at the table. It was delicious.

Everyone had an enjoyable evening and all of them left feeling very full.

***

Nick had to meet her mother as Carmen still lived at home with her.

Finally, he said to her one day on the phone that he is not going to meet her in the city as they always did, but he would come to Brooklyn to pick her up at her home.

Carmen asked him to dress down as this is Bensonhurst, and she didn't want anyone to mistake him for gay and beat him up.

The local street boys hanging out on the corner would have a field day with him if they saw him getting off the subway train on 86th street holding a purse and wearing a crystal belt buckle.

So after he closed the shop he took the train into Brooklyn and had no trouble finding her house. It was only a short half block walk and there was no incidence with the local neighborhood youth.

Carmen explained to her mother what Nick did for a living and that he had to dress real fancy for his clients. It was all a show, she explained.

Hopefully, she sent the message across to her mother. If not she would hear about it in Italian right in front of Nick.

But Nick is smart enough to bring a big box of expensive chocolates and a bouquet of flowers for her mother. When he gave them to her she smiled and said in Italian to Carmen "that was very nice of him. I did not expect that."

Anna Marie spoke perfect English but when she wanted to say something to her daughters she did not want someone else to hear, she spoke Italia to them. This is her secret language.

Nick is dressed in jeans with a white shirt and a tan corduroy jacket. His clothing is very chic and not garish or flashy. He knew this is an important meeting, and didn't want to blow it. He left his purse in Manhattan but thought that his wallet made his pants bulge and ruined the clean lines, so he only took what identification he thought would be necessary.

Eventually, after dating for a while, he asked Carmen to marry him. She said yes as she is not dating anyone else, is lonely without a man and did not have anyone else asking her out at the moment.

She knew she isn't getting any younger, and most of the girls she went to high school with already are carrying babies on their hips. Carmen realized if she wanted to have children she had to get started sooner rather than later.

So they were married in a small church ceremony with only their immediate families, and close friends present.

Carmen's close friends were three girls she went to high school with who still lived on the block, and of course Nicole. Nicole was the maid of honor at the wedding.

Nick's friends were a showcase of Manhattan chic and couture trends. Outlandish and flashy would be the key descriptive words. But everyone had a ball at the reception. It was held at Palumbo's Palace on Cropsey Avenue in their back party room. The food was homemade as usual, and the beer never stopped coming.

Palumbo's specialty is imported Italian cheese rolled in breaded eggplant and cooked in olive oil imported from their family's farm in Sicily. And the dry white Italian wine is, of course, imported also.

After the wedding, the couple moved into the basement apartment of her mother's house where her grandmother Theresa Avila had lived while she was alive.

Nick commuted to Manhattan by the subway but dressed very conservatively until he arrived at work. Then he would change into his designer clothes. He knew who hung out by the street corners in Brooklyn, and he wanted to get to work and home in one piece. Stay out of the way of the goombahs and everything would be okay.

But Nicole still had a place in Carmen's heart, even after the marriage, and they would get together every now and then as they did before. They were, after all, very special lifelong best friends forever.

Carmen took care of her apartment like her mother did for her family, and she cooked and cleaned when she went home from work. It is two bedrooms, a living room, and a small kitchen. A lot of the space on the ground floor is separated by a wall for the garage.

***

One day, about six months after their marriage, when she is putting Nick's washed clothes back in his underwear drawer she noticed some underwear in the wash that is not his, or hers. It had initials embroidered on it, and then she recognized the initials. They belonged to a male model, Thomas Stevens, who frequently stopped in at Nick's shop in Soho to buy his clothes.

Thomas was an up and coming male model. Tall, lanky, and a dirty blond, his look was in demand for a lot of photo shoots.

He grew up in the Midwest and came to New York to make it big in the modeling industry. But male models are not as in demand as the women and didn't usually make the really big money. He is struggling to make ends meet, and lived paycheck to paycheck. When he is paid it is usually big enough to carry him for a while, but not for too long.

One day when he is shopping in Soho he walked into Nick's shop to browse and saw Nick behind the counter. They made eye contact, and Nick came out to speak to him.

"Hi, welcome to my little shop of designs," Nick said to him, with an ever so slight lisp that is barely detectable.

"Thanks, you have some very unusual clothes for men. I saw them in your window, and I like them very much" Thomas responded. "I like this grey and red pinstripe suit very much. Can I try it on?"

"Of course," Nick said. "Just follow me to the back where the dressing room is."

As they walked to the back Nick picked out a black dress shirt and a fire engine red tie, with a matching red handkerchief for the breast pocket.

Once they both were in the dressing room they made eye contact again and signals were sent to each other. They slowly moved closer to each other, and then they kissed.

That is the beginning of their torrid affair. They would meet in the shop after lunch if Thomas is not working, or after it closed at night. Sometimes Nick missed the train home and called Carmen to say he is going to a fashion affair in the city.

After this Nick generously helped support him financially as the shop is starting to do very well.

A lot of big name female and male movie stars are starting to shop there, and his reputation started to grow as a designer. And Mr. Lew always made his custom designs for the stars a priority. Especially after Nick brought in one of Hollywood's leading Asian female stars to his shop to meet Mr. Lew. She started to shop at Nicks, and he made the introduction.

When Nick's line was picked up by Bergdorf's his design firm really started to grow. He had to move from the Soho shop to larger quarters in the garment center and started to hire people to help him out.

He was doing a lot of custom work now. His trademark reputation was a great design, quick turnaround, and hand delivery to his established clients.

***

It was at this moment when she saw Thomas's underwear in Nick's drawer Carmen understood her husband Nick is also bisexual. This is why they didn't have as strong a sexual relationship, after six months of marriage, as she felt they should have.

He was more interested in boys than in her, although he didn't completely stop having relations with her, just not so often.

So Nicole, who is always available, took up some of the slack in that department, but Carmen began to find herself being attracted to older men.

Her father Mario died before her marriage, and it may have been an emotional insecurity issue with her. When she would meet a more mature man who caught her eye she looked to see if he was married. She knew a married man would just be interested in the sex, and not a more permanent relationship. They would not want a divorce, and neither did she due to her religion. But sex is okay in her mind as she thought of it as a bodily function.

Finally, Carmen took a lover, Roberto, who is in his late fifties. He treated her with the attention she craved which she didn't get at home.

Carmen applied for and was accepted as a sales clerk in a major department store in downtown Brooklyn, and it was there she met Roberto.

He was an older man who is the floor sales manager, and her direct supervisor.

Roberto wore a pencil-thin mustache with flowing salt and pepper hair brushed back. He is on the thin side and not too tall, average height if one was to measure him. He spoke very well, always wore a tightly fitted three-piece suit with a flower in the lapel to work, and had an eye for the ladies even though he is married for many years.

Roberto and his wife Rosa had very close friends, Tina and Anthony, who after Anthony retired they decided to move to Florida. The brutal New York winters became too much for him to handle anymore.

What Roberto's wife Rosa did not know is that Tina and Roberto had a steady and steamy sexual affair going on for over twenty years. So when Tina moved to Florida the affair, unfortunately, came to an end, maybe.

For their vacation one summer, Rosa bought plane tickets for herself and Roberto and called Tina and Anthony they are coming for a visit.

Tina said they had an extra bedroom and insisted they had to stay with her and Anthony, not in a hotel. She said it would be more economical, and they could save a lot of money by staying with them in their condo.

They planned to go out every night for dinner and during the day see all the sights in the area together.

Which is exactly what happened except for one afternoon.

Anthony and Roberto's wife Rosa went out to the balcony of the condo which overlooked the ocean to each sit on a chaise lounge and just relaxes in the sun.

The blue ocean water seemed endless with the white sails of the ocean-going luxury yachts slowly passing by before them. There was an ever so slight breeze that blew in the smell of the ocean. They each had a sour apple martini in their hands and the Florida afternoon seemed to never end. At that moment it was pure paradise and total relaxation.

Meanwhile, Tina took Roberto by the hand, and they went into the back bedroom. They started to kiss and Tina told him how much she missed him. She rubbed her hands through his hair and she gently kissed him, and then licked his neck. Tina bent over to look out the bedroom door at the balcony to make sure they were still sitting there while Roberto had relations with her in the doorway.

When they were finished they both went out to the balcony and sat with their spouses enjoying the ocean view as if nothing had happened.

The two weeks went by very quickly, and Tina and Roberto met privately whenever they could.

Roberto is a player and when he saw Carmen in the back stock room behind the sales floor, he approached her and complimented her on her work.

"I have been noticing that you are very careful when you are out there on the sales floor. You always arrange the racks neatly, and the sweaters too, so they are stacked perfectly. That is very good, thank you," he said to her.

"I try ta-be helpful here," she answered. "I like it here. Tank you for say-in dat" Carmen answered him.

"Listen, Carmen, how would you like to grab some lunch with me on your break?" he asked.

"Soun's good. See youse at twelve, downstairs" she answered.

She was attracted to his maturity and the soft way he spoke to her. He seemed to be always around when she needed a hand with a customer or trying to reach up and put clothes on a high shelf. He was attentive to her.

At lunchtime that day they met downstairs outside the store's entrance on Fulton Street and they walked together to a small luncheonette that was nearby.

The place is crowded and a lot of people are there to pick up orders they phoned in. They quickly sat down at a small table against the wall, and Roberto pulled out a chair for her to sit down in. Nick never did that for her.

After a minute or so the waitress came over and gave them each a menu. The pages were worn from use and age, and some pages are also soiled, but the air in the place smelled delicious. Terry is the owner and short order cook, and she used tons of garlic powder in every dish she made. Her meatloaf sandwich is fantastic as she always put sautéed onions on top.

"Never look in the kitchen," Roberto told her. "The food always tastes better that way."

Carmen smiled when he said that. She thought it is clever and funny.

The waitress quickly came back to the table to take their order. She is right out of central casting, blond, very pale white skin with shocking red lipstick, and chewing gum while she took your order, and called everyone Hun.

Carmen said she would like a BLT on white toast, no mayo, and Roberto had a small cup of soup, some small butter rolls, and a coffee with cherry Danish.

"I see that you are married," Roberto said noticing her wedding ring on her hand. "How does married life feel?" he asked, testing the response she would give.

"It's okay…I guess" she answered. "It's nutting like ya see in da movies."

He sensed from her answer that she is not happily married, and he perked up a little. He saw an opening.

But he is smart enough not to be in a rush. He played it cool and calmly.

"Well maybe things will be better," Roberto told her.

Before Carmen could answer him their meal came, and they stopped talking while the waitress placed the food on the table.

"Dis is a great sam-wich," Carmen said with a mouthful of food. "Da bacon has a hick-ry taste".

"I know I have eaten it many times here before. The place doesn't look great but the food is very good" Roberto said.

"Maybe tomorrow… if we leave earlier I'll take you to Juniors, it's just down the street" Roberto said to her in a soft voice as he sipped some of his soup from the spoon.

Carmen smiled at Roberto appreciatively. She enjoyed her lunch with him as she felt that he showed genuine interest in her, in a non-threatening manner. And she has never been to Junior's and thought it sounded like a good idea. She heard about it plenty of times but had never eaten there.

The waitress came over and dropped the check on the table.

"I have it," Roberto said. "My treat, it is a pleasure to meet you informally, and hopefully we will see a lot of each other in the future".

"Dat would be nice" Carmen answered. "Tank youse for da lunch".

They stood and started to walk back to the store. On the way back to work she started to fantasize about having an affair with him. She is definitely attracted to him and enjoyed their lunch together.

She imagined their naked bodies embracing as they lay on a bed somewhere in her mind.

Fulton Street was jammed with people and the extra wide sidewalks were just wide enough to handle the sea of humanity that flowed by on it.

Later that afternoon Carmen is in the stock room opening boxes and placing shirts onto hangers on the wheeled display racks so she could transfer them to the sales floor when Roberto walked into the stockroom.

They were alone, and it is between shifts so there are not that many people working out on the sales floor yet, and nobody is in the stock room beside them.

He walked up to her and stood behind her.

"Carmen," he said, I really like you a lot. I enjoyed our lunch".

"Tanks, I like youse too," she said.

After lunch, she returned back to work and continued to dream he would make a move on her. She is physically very enamored of him. Now the daydream is about to become reality.

Roberto touched her on her shoulder and slowly turned her around. She stood there looking at him, not moving, not willing to tell him to leave her alone. She is hoping he would kiss her. Her body wanted a passionate kiss from him. Carmen slowly tilted her head slightly to the left. Roberto picked up on her body language, the signals she was sending out, and he knew what to do next.

He placed one hand on her waist and pulled her into him, lifting her chin with his other hand at the same time.

They turned their heads towards each other and slowly he kissed her, moving his right arm up from her waist and gently caressing her back.

After a moment or two in a passionate embrace, he took her into his private office behind the storage wall and locked the door.

There was a window in the office that overlooked the street six stories below. But they did not bother to look out. Very few people ever went into that office as it was hidden away out of sight. Unless you were personally taken there, even the employees forgot that it was there, or even knew of it.

They embraced again and kissed.

Tenderly he caressed her as she started to gyrate slowly and then her legs started to feel weak. Carmen's knees buckled and Roberto gently lifted her and placed her in a sitting position on his desk.

Finally, they finished and he helped her off the desk. With his pants on the floor and her skirt tucked into her waistband, they kissed standing upright. She rubbed her fingers slowly through his hair, and he held the back of her head as he kissed her with passion.

But the next shift is coming on the sales floor, and they had to sneak out quietly as if nothing had happened. Only twenty minutes had gone by, and they were both completely satisfied.

Carmen soon came to have lunch with him almost daily. Sometimes they did not bother to go out, but stayed in that small office for their lunches, as if they ate any food at all.

Carmen soon started to think about having a life with him. She could leave Nick and move in with Roberto. But she did not have the guts to do it. She had to talk to someone. She knew that married men were not eager to leave their families, but she was falling for Roberto in a big way. He was fulfilling a basic human desire that she had, and she did not want to give that up.

But divorce is unheard of in her family, and her faith frowned on it.

This is why she is in the church today to speak to the priest.

Her nerves are coming undone and she didn't know what to do. She had both a male and female lover, and she is torn between them, and her marriage vows.

Father Donovan stretched out his hand and gently took hold of hers. She felt secure enough to start telling him of her marital problems.

"Fadder, I am very confused. I am married, but I have been hav-in an affair wit an older man I woik with. My hus-ban is gay an rarely has sex wit me. An my best girl fren in the world is also my lover" Carmen told him.

"I d'own feel satisfied in my marriage. I have deese feelin's I can't control" she told him.

He understood what she was saying and where she was coming from. Maybe he understood it too well.

Father Donovan is having his own problems, and his desires are the same as hers. He stood and closed the door to his office.

He leaned over, closer to her.

Carmen is also physically attracted to him, as he is an older mature man. Perhaps she needed a father figure in her life, but there definitely is an attraction between them both.

She also leaned back into him, and finally, they kissed.

Just then Sister Bernadette knocked on the door. He stood and went to the door to talk to her. After a brief conversation, he locked the door and started to go back to his desk.

But he stopped and started to rub Carmen's shoulders again. It felt good to her. Slowly he leaned over her and kissed her again, this time on the side of her neck. His hands gently slid down the front of her blouse, under her brassiere.

Carmen stood up and faced him. She could not control her emotions, and her hormones were going full blast. Quickly she unbuttoned her blouse exposing herself.

She put her arms around his neck and they kissed. Her hand placed on the back of his head, she passionately kissed him. It seemed like forever to her that their lips were together.

They were committing a major sin in the eyes of the church. But their passion and their hormonal juices were stirring and could not be constrained.

She knew in her heart it is wrong but he is in a position of masculine authority, and she had these feelings, these longings for him, for an alpha male which needed to be fulfilled.

Her upbringing is going out the window at that very moment, and she didn't care.

The Church is not going to hold her back from her desires. And she acted on them.

That lustful afternoon lasted for a long time. And it became a standing weekly appointment for "counseling" for her at the church.

The truth of the matter is she never went back to mass again after that afternoon.

But she did meet with Father Donovan every week in his office.

This went on for a long time.

Chapter 13 -

Finally, the day came when Paulie announced he finally is going to Florida, and Rocco is going to be the go-to guy in his absence. In reality, this is happening already for almost two years. Paulie is spending more and more time in Florida, and Rocco is handling his affairs in New York.

He calls Rocco one morning to meet him on the corner of McDonald Avenue and Avenue U at about one in the afternoon.

They casually walked to Pauli's favorite Italian restaurant which is nearby, and together they go inside to enjoy a late lunch.

Paulie orders the balsamic veal with grilled vegetables, and Rocco has his usual lunch, a shrimp parm sandwich with extra Italian gravy [spaghetti source].

After they are finished eating Paulie sits back and gives a heavy sigh. He is tired.

"Rocco" Paulie said to him "let's go fa a walk." They stood, Paulie, left a hundred dollar bill on the table, and they walked out onto McDonald Avenue.

The trains are screeching above them as they talked. It is hard to hear, and this is why they usually talked under the elevated trains.

"I am getting too old fa dis anymore," he told Rocco as they walked along 86th Street. "I am gonna go ta Florida an I want you ta be in charge fa me. Call da guys an I am gonna throw a big dinner fa everyone and tell dem dat you are the go-to guy from now on".

"D'own worry bout nut-tin," Rocco told him. I will take care of da details".

To celebrate his "official retirement without having been killed or jailed" Paulie asked Rocco to arrange for a big dinner reception at a local catering hall in Brooklyn. Paulie invited everyone who is important both to him, and Rocco to come.

The hall is in South Brooklyn and has a marble entryway with large brass and crystal chandeliers. The glass doors to the hall are massive with solid brass handles that extended almost the entire length of the door. It reeked of classless money and opulence.

The owners of the catering hall are two brothers who grew up in Bensonhurst with Paulie. What no one knew is Paulie is the money man behind the hall, and he used it to launder his illegal cash. Catering halls deal in just enough declared money to make it seem legit. But they skim tons of cash off the top. Their customers pay with the cash they hid from the government, and the catering halls keep most of it undeclared when they receive it in payment for a party.

The reception is set for seven o'clock on a Saturday evening, and there is free valet parking and an open bar once you walk inside to the hall.

Rocco had reserved a few tables for his family, and some for his business associates.

He is there with Gina Marie. Gina Marie's sisters sat with her at her table. Their children sat at another table with all their cousins, and Antony and Frank are with their girlfriends.

When Frank walked in with Juanita Rocco thought he recognized her from the brothel over the candy store on 86th street from years ago. But he wasn't sure. She looked just like the young Puerto Rican girl Bernardo hid in his shoe store, but older, more mature, and had a fuller body. He just stared at her for a long minute, until he was almost positive that he recognized her.

Rocco expected her to keep her mouth shut, and not say anything to Gina Marie. He had fooled around with her very often in the brothel for so many years before and had completely forgotten about her until now. She is just one of many. He is a little confused that Frank is here with her.

But this was years ago. Maybe she wouldn't recognize him. But she is very attractive, and he had primal urges he couldn't control, or ever did.

Anthony arrived with Basha and sat down next to Frank.

Mary Catherine came in with Irwin and found Gina Marie's table and sat next to her sister.

Also invited were some business associates and friends, including Victor and Olga. They sat at the other end of the room with the Philadelphia people.

Last to arrive was Carmen and Nick, to keep appearances up she brought him. She also sat at the table with her sisters.

The family priest came in a little while later and sat with Rocco and his family. Father Donovan almost had a heart attack when he realized that he was attending a dinner party with Basha and Carmen. As he sat down he started to sweat realizing that he could be exposed if they said anything. His career flashed before his eyes. Yes, he took chances with, but he never socialized with them, let alone two at the same time.

Basha is just as startled when she saw him sit down at the table. She hoped he didn't say anything. She hadn't been with him for a few months now. Basha is enjoying a new life with Anthony and stopped visiting the priest, although she still saw Hamilton on occasion at a motel near Kennedy airport.

Flustered, and to calm her nerves she started to drink sour apple martinis, on an empty stomach.

Carmen also didn't know that Rocco would invite the priest to the party…and to their table yet. She felt both uncomfortable and happy at the same time when she saw him. It didn't matter to her that Nick is there, but she did want to maintain the illusion of a marriage in front of her sisters.

As she sat down Juanita glanced over to the main table and recognized Rocco. She knew who he is, but didn't realize how he is related to Frank. But she knew better than to say anything. She started to drink whiskey sours to calm her jitters. The catering hall only used top-shelf liquor, not the cheap nameless stuff, and she is starting to feel no pain from the booze.

The waitress that night serving the main table is Nicole who worked there part-time to supplement her income. She usually is able to take home a lot of leftovers when an affair is finished, both in food and men.

Now Carmen sat back and realized she has her husband, her lover the priest, and her lesbian lover there also. She also started to drink to calm her nerves.

This is going to be some dinner party.

**

The live five-piece band started to play music, and the conversations were muted due to the loud music, although they did not stop.

Most affairs make it difficult to talk over the loud music. That is just how it is. The bandleader took the microphone and started to sing in Italian.

People left their seats and started to dance in the middle of the social hall on the beautifully stained oak parquet floor.

The waiters brought around trays of garlic chicken on a small spit, and other finger foods to each table.

Everyone is having a great time.

When the music slowed and everyone is seated the first course, a fruit salad, is being brought out to the tables. The music started again, and people ate, then a few people stood to dance again.

After finishing the fruit salad Juanita excused herself and arose to go to the powder room downstairs. She had to go to the bathroom as she had a lot of liquid refreshment in her, and had to relieve herself.

Rocco is sitting at the next table and saw her get up, excused himself, and followed her downstairs where the restrooms are located.

He had to satisfy his curiosity about her. When they walked to the bottom of the steps, Rocco called out to her "hey Star".

Juanita stopped.

She now knew he knew who she is.

That is the name she used many years ago when she was a prostitute in the Brooklyn bordello run by Big Sally.

But Rocco is very gentlemanly.

"Lis-sen Star, I see dat youse are here wit my neph-few Frank. I w'own say nut-thin course I d'own wan ta hurt his feel-ins. But I do expect youse to repay my kindness to youse" he told her.

It was many years before that he brought her into the bordello, and he did not forget her now.

He saw Frank liked her and otherwise he knew he would not have brought her here tonight. But it would have to cost her something to keep quiet, and he wanted his payment right then and now.

"For old time's sake," Rocco insisted, as they slipped into the catering manager's office, and closed the door. This is to be her payment for silence. She knew he now owned her as long as she is with Frank.

Rocco threw the pillows off the expensive gold gilded rococo burgundy leather sofa that was in the office and had her lay down on it. Before she did she hiked up the bottom of her dress over her hips as she sat down and then she raised her legs in the air, waiting for him.

She then paid him his price for his silence.

Rocco is older now, past middle age, and he has trouble being intimate. She serviced him in another way.

Satisfied, he told her not to worry that her secret was safe with him. But she knew better. She had dealt with his type before and knew this, tonight, was just a down payment on his continued silence.

Upstairs Basha stood, and a little tipsy went to go to the ladies room. Father Donovan stood and excused himself from the table to follow her downstairs.

As Basha is walking down the hall to the ladies room Father Donovan called out to her just before she was to go into the restroom, and they stopped to talk.

"I am happy to see you here Basha," Father Donovan told her. "I did not know that you were seeing Anthony."

She looked at him and smiled with her big blue doe eyes. He knew what that meant. Basha is embarrassed to tell him before that she won't see him anymore, so she just stopped coming to the church. But she never could say no.

He took hold of her hand and looked around. There is no one else downstairs that he could see. The hallway is empty.

"Come with me" he whispered to her and led her into the family restroom under the rear hallway. There he closed the door, locked it, and embraced her passionately.

Basha did not resist. Her primal urges and the alcohol worked together to bring down any denials of the situation she might have had, or if she ever had any.

They had a quick sexual encounter in the family restroom. It had been a few months since they were together and he was making up for lost time.

When he was finished she stood up and smiled at him.

Then she kissed him, passionately, shoving her tongue down his throat.

Father Donovan held her and told her he was very happy to see her again, and he had truly missed her. She readily agreed she missed him also, and told him when they were finished, and she was cleaning herself up she would call him next week so they could get together again.

She missed his masculine attention. He made her feel wanted and needed.

Afterwards, when everyone is finished with their encounters they all went back quietly, one by one, to their seats before the main meal came out, as if nothing had happened.

***

The soup is being brought out, and everybody is back in his or her seats. The dancing stopped, and the band started to play soft soothing music to dine by.

Quietly the bus boys came around for the first time to clear the fruit plates, and help with the soup bowls.

The bus boy for Basha's table is a young Jamaican man in his twenties that Basha recognized. He was one of Hamilton's buddies she had met a year before at his apartment.

Basha slept with Hamilton only two weeks before in a motel room near Kennedy Airport. She casually mentioned to him, before having a torrid intimate session, when the conversation slowed down her friend Juanita told her Anthony mentioned Frank knew who killed his father, but she didn't know any names.

To her, it is small talk to kill some time as they undressed each other in the motel room near Kennedy Airport.

They rarely talked about anything of substance. Sex is the only real reason he is with her. And she is with him because he filed an emotional void in her life.

But as she said it Hamilton froze for a second. He stood motionless and started to think about what she just told him. Basha did not notice anything.

At that exact moment, he realized he is a marked man. He needed to take action, or he would end up like his dead gang members in that Brooklyn basement.

***

Before Basha could say hello to the busboy he took out a pistol from his waistband and fired at point-blank range.

He shot Frank in the back of the head. Then he turned his gun on Basha and shot at her from across the table with two shots. He realized she recognized him. From the force of the bullets, she is pushed back away from the table, and her body hit the wall behind her. She fell to the floor fatally wounded.

The other Jamaican busboy took out his gun when the shooting started. His target is Paulie and Rocco.

Hamilton is tying up loose ends tonight.

The busboy then turned and tried to run out the rear door into a waiting car where Hamilton is waiting for his men in the rear parking lot.

But he had to pass Olga's table. She and Viktor were sitting near the exit.

Upon hearing the gunshots Olga stood up and extended her arms with her Glock pointing at the fleeing busboy. He saw her and turned towards her quickly raising his gun and tried to aim it at her. But he was only a fraction of a second too late.

Two shots rang out. He is propelled backward with two bullets to the center of his chest. His knees buckled, and he dropped to the dance floor with such impact he let go of his gun as he fell. It slid away onto the dance floor, away from his curled up body. It is rare when Olga missed a shot.

The second Jamaican busboy that is there also started to withdraw his gun. When the shooting started he is killed instantly. He was about to start shooting at Rocco and Paulie after he saw the other busboy shoot at Frank and Basha. That was the plan.

But Hamilton did not plan on Frank being shot so early. The plan was to kill Frank when the main course was served, and everyone is seated and eating. They would all be in their seats and easy targets.

Paulie's men always packed heat wherever they went. If you looked at their suits you could see a bulge by their shoulder or their waist. That night there are a lot of bulges at Paulie's private farewell party.

Jimmy the Basket is standing behind Paulie talking to his date when he heard the shots at the next table. He did not fumble as he pulled his suit jacket back, and took out his gun. Jimmy the Basket shot the busboy as he stood in front of Paulie's table.

The busboy fell to the floor behind Paulie's chair grimacing in pain, but still alive. He is shot in the right arm, and once in his chest. One shot missed as Jimmy the Basket is not known as a marksman from any distance other than two feet away. He is used to shooting his gun when it is at the back of someone's head, not fifteen feet away.

Beanball quickly stood and ran over to the wounded busboy lying on the floor writhing in pain. With all his might he forcefully stomped on the kid's throat once, twice, three times until he was sure he broke his neck, and he saw blood spurting out of the large open gash on his throat. The busboy gasped a few times for air, and then just lay there motionless.

People started to run out the doors, the women holding tightly onto their furs, and leaving their checked coats. They could always go back to get them eventually. But right now they had to leave before the police arrived.

***

Father Donovan stood and started to administer last rites to Basha. Her breathing is heavy and labored. Anthony quickly knelt down next to her and raised her up in his arms, holding her close to him.

She turned her head away from the priest as he is praying, and looked into Anthony's eyes. A smile crossed her lips, and as she tried to say "I love you" to him she expired. She died in his arms, probably one of the only men she had ever really loved.

Bedlam had broken out in the hall. People are running everywhere trying to get away when the shooting started. Panic broke out as the guests ran out onto the street.

Hamilton is still waiting outside in the getaway car. When he heard the shots, and none of his men ran outside he drove away when he saw Paulie's henchmen come running out with their guns drawn.

The drug war is on again, but this time Hamilton is alone. All his buddies are dead.

He drove away and went to LaGuardia airport, and parked in the long-term lot. Then he calmly took the shuttle to the airport and bought a ticket to Jamaica which is leaving shortly. He is going to start over with his old contacts in Kingston.

***

The police never figured out who shot whom that night. The guns, the people who did the shooting, and guest list disappeared immediately. The caterer knew better than to call the police until certain people left the premises.

Then he first called for an ambulance. Waited ten minutes, and then called the police to report gunshots.

When the police arrived he said he was in the kitchen and saw nothing, as were his waiters. The police are told that the dead Jamaican busboys were out in the banquet hall at that time. They were supposed to pick up the fruit dishes and bring them back to the kitchen. He did not know what went on in the hall, and he only heard the gunshots, never seeing who used the guns in the main hall.

The police are informed it was a private party, and a fictitious name is given for the host. The caterer said he was paid in cash for the event, and he did not know anything else.

Certain police captains from Brooklyn are generously taken care of, and the shooting never hit the newspapers. Soon the shooting is forgotten and became a cold case never to be solved.

***

A few weeks after the party things returned back to a somewhat normal pace.

Carmen continued visiting with Father Donovan whenever she went to church on her day off, and she also still slept with Nicole and Roberto on other days, times, and when she felt the need.

She needed Father Donovan's mature comfort, and security, as she is still having trouble with her marriage to Nick.

After another year of her sexual meetings with Father Donovan, they had a heart to heart talk one afternoon in the church basement.

Carmen entered his office as she had done so many times before, and she locked the door once she was inside.

Father Donovan embraced her in his arms and she felt the strength and comfort she always desired.

She tilted her head upwards as he slowly kissed her on the lips, nuzzling his way to her slender neck. She felt the passion rising in the room, and started to unbutton her blouse.

But this time he stopped her. Gently taking her hand he placed it on his heart and told her, for the first time, that he loved her.

"Carmen I have to stop living a lie. I cannot go on like this. My conscience has started to bother me every time I think of you. I have made a decision to leave the church. Will you come live with me, and leave Nick?"

She had never expected this.

Stunned she stood there silently trying to absorb what was just said to her.

This is more than the good sex and emotional security blanket she enjoyed and craved. This is now becoming real to her. A major decision faced and had to be made.

She went to sit in the old leather chair in his office when she saw the crucifix hanging behind his desk chair. She had never noticed it before, it was just background decoration, although she had been in his office weekly for their trysts for years. But now what the two of them had been doing became reality to her.

It was at that moment she realized she had to decide if she wanted to bring back into her life the parochial teachings she had ignored, or forget them, and move on with him. The opportunity of a mature man finally giving himself to her totally began to seep in.

She knew that if she lived with him she had to forget her romps with Nicole, even though she had enjoyed them ever since she was a teenager. And her job in downtown Brooklyn would have to be dropped also. Roberto would become past history, and in the future only appear in her dreams.

What would her mother say, her sisters too? She never emotionally thought of Nick, but how a divorce would affect her standing in the church suddenly became so clear to her.

These things quickly spun through her mind as she tried to make a decision to commit to him or not.

Deep in the dark bowels of the church, after patiently waiting so many years, would the evil one finally conquer one more soul?

Slowly Carmen stood and put her arms around his neck. Ever so gently, with tears slowly rolling down her cheeks, she stroked the back of his hair and tenderly kissed him.

Carmen had made her decision.

238

***

Nick eventually decided he would separate from Carmen, and then get a divorce. But right now for monetary reasons, he kept the false front of a marriage going.

He is making a lot of money as a designer for the stars, and a divorce would be oh so expensive he thought. Maybe later, maybe not, but not right now, why rock the boat until he had to make the final decision.

A few months later he moved in with some guy he met in the village off of Washington Square. He had broken off with the male model and finally came out of the closet. But he was still married to Carmen although in name only. As long as she did not ask for a divorce he was not about to either.

***

Juanita, after the party, immediately went back to Park Slope in a taxi and packed all her clothes. Meanwhile, Rocco stood on the sidewalk outside the caterers thinking of his next move. What Juanita could not fit in a suitcase she threw into black garbage bags and called for a car service.

She moved out of Frank's condo that night and moved into a women's shelter in Manhattan. Juanita left her key to the apartment on a table, took what little cash is in the condo and locked the door from the rear of the door handle, and did not look back. No note, no nothing. She disappeared into the New York mass of humanity, and no one ever heard from her again.

She left her job the next day by not bothering to show up for work. It did not take her long to find a new position as a receptionist. She is working for another law firm which is located in the financial district, not uptown, and she never heard from Rocco or anyone from that group again.

Juanita knew she had to get away from "them" or she would never have a chance at any kind of normal life. She is a survivor.

As an experienced good looking receptionist she had little difficulty getting a new position. She is going to start over again as she did before, and never once ever thought of contacting anyone from Frank's family.

Eventually, she met and married a much older, retired lawyer from the new law firm where she worked. He was a senior partner whose wife had died a few years before. He was lonely and took an immediate liking to her when he came into the office and saw her sitting in the lobby. Soon he asked her out for dinner. She knew what the score is and gladly accepted a date with him. She hoped and planned if she played her cards right he would be hers.

After a few months of dating, and a prenuptial agreement they both signed, they were married in Las Vegas on a weeklong trip they took to Nevada

He lived on Park Avenue in a multimillion-dollar duplex condo with a butler and housekeeper.

His chauffer took both of them to where ever they wanted to go, and she is now a regular shopper at Bergdorf Goodman. She especially likes their perfumes and body oils which made her smell sensuous for her husband. Finally, she is living the good life, she had survived the streets.

When her husband finally retired from the law firm and cashed out, Juanita and her husband decided to move to Florida. They sold their luxury condo on Park Avenue. Then bought waterfront property in Coral Gables Florida, and lived a life of luxury in the Florida sun.

She wore diamonds, drove a top of the line Mercedes, ate out almost every day, and her husband always wore a big smile in the morning.

***

The death of Frank weighted heavily on Mary Catherine, and she couldn't bear to stay in the area any longer. She is depressed and again felt she needed a change of scenery. She had to get out of Brooklyn, New York City, and away from all the madness.

She lost her husband, and now her son to violence. Enough is enough, and she is getting very depressed.

Mary Catherine asked Irwin to sell their business.

He is older now and had enough of the daily grind. He agreed, and they moved to Santa Fe, New Mexico. He used Metropolitan Business Advisors Inc. to sell his two locations, and they found a buyer who gave him a lot of money.

Irwin and Mary Catherine bought a house just outside of Santa Fe on the edge of the desert, yet just minutes from downtown. She wanted to get as far away from Brooklyn as she could.

Mary Catherine liked living in Santa Fe as it has a quaint feel to it, is just artsy enough, is near Taos, and the artist community there. She felt at peace when she walked in the quiet desert every morning at sunrise.

She begged Anthony to come with her, but he is making big money now working for Rocco and wouldn't go with her. He did not have the attitude, or aptitude, that Frank had so he is kept working inside on construction paperwork, and not going out collecting or making deals.

He missed Basha and mourned for her. He never knew the running around she had done with Hamilton or Father Donovan. Someday he hoped he would meet another girl that he could love.

But right now he is not looking for anyone.

***

Two years passed since the private party.

Rocco is older now, a little slower, but still, is doing his thing for Paulie. He is taking orders over the phone, in code, from him as Paulie now lives in Tampa.

Then one sunny morning a private plane landed at Teterboro Airport in Teterboro New Jersey. It flew in from the Caribbean during the night.

When it taxied to the terminal three black SUV's with tinted windows were waiting. They were new recruits who flew up a week before the private plane landed. The SUV's are filled with guns.

The door to the jet opened and Hamilton walked down the steps from the plan, and into one of the waiting SUV's.

Once he is inside he told the driver "take us to Bensonhurst an I'm gonna…."

The End

This novel is based on a flash fiction story from the author's previous novel "People Stories in 600 Words, as told by a raconteur."

The character Olga is brought back in a later novel "Hot Cash/Cold Bodies." The main heroine in this book is a female detective named Khara Bennet who is caught in a life or death struggle with a Mexican drug cartel. Olga is brought in to assist her.

It is a fast-paced page burning crime/adventure novel.

Due to its fan base requests, a sequel followed. "Khara Bennet ---Vengeance" is the follow-up novel.

The third novel in the trilogy is "Dead Girls Don't Die".

www.CreativeFiction.net

www.ingramcontent.com/pod-product-compliance
Lightning Source LLC
Chambersburg PA
CBHW061007280326
41935CB00009B/868